SNAPS, SECRETS AND STORIES FROM MY LIFE

# Sheila:
## Snaps, Secrets and

With very
special love
to Johathan...
from
Sheila S.

# Scotter
## Stories from My Life

RANDOM HOUSE
AUSTRALIA

Random House Australia Pty Ltd
20 Alfred Street, Milsons Point, NSW 2061
http://www.randomhouse.com.au

Sydney   New York   Toronto
London   Auckland   Johannesburg
and agencies throughout the world

First published 1998
Copyright © Sheila Scotter

National Library of Australia
Cataloguing-in-Publication Data

Scotter, Sheila
Sheila Scotter : snaps, secrets and stories from my life.

ISBN 0 09 183543 7

1. Scotter, Sheila. 2. Fashion editors – Australia – Biography. I. Title.

746 92092
Designed by Guy Mirabella
Typeset by Lynne Hamilton
Printed by Griffin Press Pty Ltd, South Australia

10 9 8 7 6 5 4 3 2 1

# Foreword

Now, how does one write about the seriously stellar Sheila
Scotter! An awesome task. The Silver Duchess herself?
Impossible. But in a moment of weakness, strolling with her
down Little Bourke Street in Melbourne I find I have agreed.

So here goes ...

A life that has travelled from Calcutta to boarding
school in England at an early age—four, no less—to fashion;
to her work at the age of 28 as a buyer for imported clothes
with the Myer Emporium in Melbourne; to the final plum in
the fashion world here, her appointment as editor of *Vogue*
Australia and *Vogue* New Zealand. This connection with
high fashion has been there throughout her life, either pro-
fessionally or through her own persona.

It was in this post in Sydney as *Vogue* editor in the six-
ties that I first became aware of Sheila Scotter. Whether we
actually met then I cannot be sure, but I certainly knew of
her. *Vogue* journalists would sometimes be dispatched to
interview the odd actor, and certainly Sir Tyrone Guthrie's
production of King Oedipus would have brought me a little
nearer the 'presence'. Quite frankly, I was in awe of the
woman, mildly terrified, I think. The usual epithets and
phrases for the highly successful preceded her everywhere—
formidable, imperious, forthright, not one to suffer fools

gladly. What I did know was that she ran a superb organisation that produced a seriously classy magazine.

The Vogue days ended in 1971 and Sheila vanished from the Australian scene. Her return in the eighties to Melbourne coincided with a radical change in my professional life. I began to visit Melbourne with plays from the Sydney Theatre Company, joint Sydney Theatre Company/Melbourne Theatre Company productions and, once or twice, Melbourne Theatre Company productions. It was over those years of working in Melbourne that I finally met Sheila. Many, many times. And we became friends. Because among all her other characteristics, Sheila is a passionate lover and supporter of the Arts and an unselfconscious friend of, and advocate for, all performers. This entertaining book describes how influential and invaluable her help and affection has been. She is a superb committee member and has been instrumental in raising enormous sums for the Arts. She is indefatigable. All this is documented.

But I want to speak about the Sheila who is my friend. Images here. Catching Sheila unawares at the reception desk in the apartments where I stay in Melbourne, handing over a present for opening night. She is like a child caught in a guilty act, giggling almost. The gift is perfect. Teas, biscuits, goodies in a basket accompanied by the card written in the unmistakable, bold hand. Every time I open in Melbourne, similar treats are delivered! Sheila presiding over the Columnists' Club luncheons in Melbourne, of which entertaining group she insisted I become an honorary member.

Lunch at Sheila's perfect and utterly relaxing flat in Albert Park. How she loves her 'French' quarter of Melbourne.

Always one or two 'chums' willingly ordered up. She is relaxed and yes, sometimes, mildly bossy as a hostess. Earlier, lunches in the converted stable in South Yarra that housed her for a time. The image is always black and white. Striking. Straight. Yes, now that I think of it, straight is the word to apply to Sheila … talking, walking, dealing, persuading. All done 'straight'. No deviation from the impeccable standard that was set, perhaps, all those years ago in the cradle in Calcutta when an unwavering Good Fairy wafted over.

In an, at times, ungenerous world, Sheila's generosity is like a beacon. Her enthusiasm for performers in all fields is legendary. Her manners are impeccable. Always a hand-written thank-you card to the company the day after an opening night. Encouraging, even when the performance may have been less than lustrous. The only criticisms must always be constructive. Amongst the forthrightness, then, dwells one of the kindest people I know.

How strange to think that this same Sheila who spiked a flick of mild terror all those years ago should have become the most trusted, the most lovable of friends. Well not strange at all really. No wonder she is surrounded by us all.

Ruth Cracknell

# Acknowledgements

I received great kindness from a few special people during the writing of this book. I am deeply indebted to Sally Moss whom I quickly nick-named 'the tag lady'. Sally was responsible for editing the manuscript, and from time to time would take away a few of my typed chapters to read. Back they would come with little tags on some of the pages with neatly written suggestions for improvement ... 'you have already implied this' or 'readers will want to know more about him or her' and so on. I would often argue with her but Sally usually won ... and for that I am now jolly grateful. If I write another book I would definitely ask for her sound advice. She is the best and I loved working with her.

The designer of the book was Guy Mirabella with whom I also enjoyed working (even when he refused to give me more space for captions to the many snaps he selected!). His multi-talents were so appreciated and he has done me proud ... if he will pardon the expression.

Not only do I feel honoured to have the name of Ruth Cracknell on the cover, but I owe her a special debt of gratitude. This busy lady read the manuscript and wrote the foreword during a particularly tiring time ... rehearsing, acting as well as promoting her own fascinating book *A Biased Memoir* (A best seller? You bet!). So an enormous thank-you to dearest Ruth Cracknell.

Sheila Scotter 1998

# Contents

# Before I Begin ...

Any woman of *'un certain age'* (as the French so elegantly describe anyone over seventy) has a past. And unless one has a past there is hardly any point in writing an autobiography.

This book has come about through the constant nag-nagging of a few close chums. Some of them have been my confidants in times of trouble and stress, others have shared in happy and successful times. Some have merely heard me chattering on about certain happenings in my long life. 'Why don't you write your autobiography?' was the question they asked me umpteen times. My reply? 'I'm too busy this year and too lazy.' Besides I would only want to do it my way—it couldn't be all stiff and stodgy.

I felt quiet daunted by the challenge, especially since I am by nature not someone who analyses at great length. I had in mind an assortment of memories, anecdotal snippets, some secrets, some snaps ... Readers would of course find out where I had been born and when, where I had been educated, whether I had ever married, what sort of a career I had had, and they would even get to approve or disapprove of my romantic liaisons, but nothing was to be chronographic. I knew I would be criticised for being selective—but that was my prerogative. If we cannot preside over our own life story, what *can* we preside over?

I was told to get myself a good literary agent and talk to him or her about my ideas. Eventually I did this. I approached only one—Anthony Williams in Sydney. He had so many prominent people on his list of clients that I was doubtful that my kind of autobiography, or rather the way I wished to write it, would appeal to him. It did.

Tony told me there and then that he knew a publisher who might be interested. Within only a few days (this guy moves quickly) it was arranged.

It was the publisher's suggestion to start with my seventieth birthday. 'Why not?' I thought, and I began to make notes. Hence the beginning of Sheila Scotter's anecdotal memoirs ...

**1**

One should never make one's début with a scandal. One should reserve that to give interest to one's old age.

**Oscar Wilde**

# Thursday's Child

I love birthdays and for a good many years I have always managed to celebrate mine in some form or another. In childhood, of course, parents or grandparents arranged the parties. At boarding school it was not exactly easy to celebrate in style—but, if you were lucky, Matron would pretend that she never knew about secret dormitory festivities after 'lights out'. During my career days I always endeavoured to take the entire day off work to celebrate, and generally succeeded.

At each celebration I have declared my age. Over the years I have often been criticised for this but never by the opposite sex. I recall being amused when my details were to be entered in the 1970 edition of *Who's Who in Australia*. The form that one had to complete, giving certain particulars for the publishers, stated that '*Ladies* were not obliged to write their date of birth if they did not wish to do so.' How quaint, I thought to myself as I filled in '2 December 1920'. I remember, too, being quite unpopular with a few women in Sydney when I admitted to being fifty while broadcasting on ABC radio 2BL. 'You are stupid to publicise your age,' I was told. I figured that perhaps those who were my contemporaries (or, dare I say, even older than myself?) had been eliminating four or five years somewhere along the line. I still maintain that any woman (or man) plagued with worry about growing older wastes an awful lot of nervous energy—and energy is something one definitely needs to conserve. This is a tip I pass on to anyone creeping towards my age group!

A great deal of energy went into the planning of my seventieth birthday party, none of it mine. Six of my closest and much loved friends formed a committee and used their combined energy, plus organising skills, to arrange a superlative dinner dance. Dulcie Boling, Douglas Butler, Margaret Darling, Glen-Marie Frost, Bill Haffenden, and John Truscott invited people 'To dress in black and white and come to a gala dinner dance in the Grand Dining Room of the Windsor Hotel Melbourne on Saturday 1 December to celebrate the 70th birthday of our mutual friend Sheila Scotter.' The gilt edged invitations also stated: 'Contributions $70, definitely no presents, 7.30pm for 8pm, black tie, and rsvp by 1/11/90 on the enclosed card'. I was strictly forbidden to have anything to do with the planning, except in providing names and addresses of those I wanted to celebrate with me. This I did, and later I was told that 140 had accepted.

Any reader who knows me personally, or who has heard of my reputation for being a bit of a perfectionist, will understand my frustration. A big party in my honour with no input from me? Frankly I felt slightly put out. Occasionally I would telephone Douglas Butler or Dulcie Boling to see how things were going, and to ask whether there was *anything* I could do to help. 'We're not telling you a thing, Scotter. Everything is going to be a surprise for you, and we all know what we are doing, thank you' was all I got for an answer. When I persevered with Douglas, who had worked under me (if you will pardon the expression), in organising many fundraising events for the Victoria State Opera and the VSO Foundation in the early 1980s, he said 'Listen, you keep telling me that you taught me all I know. So why are you worrying? Everything will be perfect on the night.'

A particular worry I had was the possibility of a ballroomful of voices singing (if one can call it a song) 'Happy Birthday to You'. I have an aversion to this wretched tune. The one time it sounded pleasant to me was when, on television years ago, I heard Marilyn Monroe sing it solo, and so seductively, to President Kennedy in the White House.

After a good many cunningly implied hints that the party was to have an all-red theme, I allowed John Truscott to persuade me to wear a bright red dress (designed by John Cavill, and described later in this book). As I had not seen the wording on the invitations, my first surprise was to find that everyone else was dressed in my favourite colours: black and white.

More surprises were to come; but Douglas was right, my early worries had been totally unnecessary. This really was what I call a 'humdinger' of a party. As guests entered the Windsor's elegant old grand dining room, champagne was offered immediately and a group of musicians was playing. Shiny black white-ribboned menus standing on candelabra-lit tables were headed:

'THURSDAY'S CHILD HAS FAR TO GO'

Miss Sheila Scotter MBE

born 2.30am

Thursday 2/12/1920

Eden Hospital, Calcutta, Bengal, India

and then set out the Order of the Evening. My second surprise was the discovery that a special friend, the Rolls-Royce of radio broadcasters, Alan Jones of 2UE Sydney, was the master of ceremonies. After welcoming everyone, Alan later introduced another surprise: one of my favourite opera singers, Geoffrey Chard, whom I have loved and admired for many years, had also flown down from Sydney. This famous baritone sang a group of love songs to *me*. Believe me, this was quite an emotional experience for one who had just reached three score years and ten. I had tears in my eyes.

Suffice to say that the food was scrumptious, the wine delectable, the music delightful, and the atmosphere fun—festive—as I have already said a humdinger of an evening. After the main course, Alan Jones called upon my (adopted) godson Bill Haffenden to propose a toast. As his speech gives a potted version of a good slice of my life, I want to share it with you, in spite of the inevitable jokes at my expense. This is what he said:

My New South Welsh expatriate, Queensland Master of Ceremonies, New South Wales immigrants, Queensland immigrants, Victorians, old Victorians, very old Victorians:

Might I begin by thanking our Master of Ceremonies for his kind introduction and, by way of retaliation, advise that during the course of the evening I overheard one lady observe in respect of our Master of Ceremonies, 'Hasn't John Laws put on some weight!'

Might I also say, Mr Chard, you Sir are a very hard act to follow.

We gather in the Windsor Hotel in this most regal dining room for our most regal guest of honour [...]

Before I first met Sheila, I had heard her spoken about in reverence, irreverence, in love, fear and occasionally terror. My first meeting arose through another very beautiful lady, Judy Potts (née Barraclough), who advised me that I must meet her and should give her a ring when she was next in Australia. During the course of this conversation a drunk slumped in the corner said 'Yeah, you'll have to catch her between hairdressing appointments.' I then telephoned Sheila and said 'Good morning, Miss Scotter. It's Bill Haffenden phoning', to which she responded 'Who are you?' I said I was a friend of Judy Potts and she promptly said 'Well you'll have to phone back. I'm just rushing off to a hairdressing appointment.'

Judy Potts had told me that I would either love her or hate her. Leo Schofield had said 'You will either love her or hate her.' Others have said that you will either love her or hate her. But if there is one thing that is so terribly clear about this evening is that 140 people have gathered in this place to say that 'We love her.'

It was hard when first seeing her this evening not to notice 'that' red dress. It's as if she has gone through some form of belated change of life. It's a strange event, as for years I thought she was either a member of a very large family suffering from some form of genetic terminal illness and by reason thereof in constant mourning, or she was the honorary patron of the Greek Widows' Association.

I have been given strict instructions about how long I am to speak for this evening. I find it difficult to squeeze some seventy years into a few minutes and accordingly I have decided to save time in at least one huge area—therefore I won't be discussing her marriages, which should reduce the content of this address very substantially.

Sheila was born in India of a family that had given service to their country and their Church by commitment to the armed forces and the Church of England. She was educated in England and during the war decided that Winston Churchill could not win World War II by himself and thus enrolled in the Royal College of Aeronautical Engineering;

thereafter she has been known to brag that she won the Battle of Britain singlehandedly. This is not exactly the background one would normally expect to have provided the foundation for what followed in the next forty-five to fifty years.

Yet, when one analyses her behaviour, one can't help but realise that the genes of the Scotter family must run heavy in her blood, producing a person with an incredible level of military precision and efficiency.

I have seen her in restaurants devour clumsy waiters as an entrée, order absolutely everyone else's courses notwithstanding their desire to the contrary, then order out of the restaurant a family who had had the stupidity to bring a young child with them.

I have seen her at the opera kill with the effectiveness of an SAS officer in order to tear herself to the front of the queue. I have seen her have directors of the largest Boards in this country eat out of her hands, and then pay her absolutely anything to make sure that she never comes back again. To this effect we are indeed all grateful to Westpac Banking Corporation for lending us Douglas Butler—one of their better loans. Poor, long suffering Douglas Butler. Dragged along to absolutely everything, bossed about, told what to do and either too polite or simply just too frightened to fight back. I have seen Sheila storm into a meeting like the Armada in full flight and depart leaving a vacuum in her wake. I have seen her order a boyfriend to remove the garbage from her house before having the opportunity of being introduced to him. On one celebrated occasion, I recall asking her whether she had ever had an affair with a particular high ranking government official or any of his predecessors, to which her response was—'In or out of office?'

Having seen Audrey from 'To the Manor Born' do precisely the same thing a week before, I saw her descend from the *Southern Aurora* in a mink, stroll down the platform and thank some bewildered foreign cleaner in the engineers section for a lovely trip.

When Scotter organises anything, there is nothing left to chance.
[...] Her efficiency and competence have seen her achieve much. She
started her career as a model and I don't think she has ever really stopped
being one. She worked at Myer and at Georges, headed the Marketing
Division in both Sydney and Paris for Joseph Bancroft, and (for the benefit of the ill-informed journalist writing in this morning's paper) headed
*Vogue* in Australia, is a worldwide-acknowledged broadcaster, columnist
and author, and more recently a person who has made an enormous contribution in this nation to opera and the arts. The young love her and
women in their twenties and thirties admire and model themselves on
her. By example, we had a young receptionist on our floor recently who
made Sir Les Patterson look like Sir John Gielgud. I can recall that Sheila
had terrorised her over the telephone on a number of occasions, making
her spell Sheila's name back to her on no less than four occasions. After
Sheila had visited our chambers, the receptionist, initially filled with fear,
told me afterwards that she wanted to be exactly like her and, I'm sorry
Dulcie Boling, she discarded her *New Idea* immediately, started reading
a *Vogue* magazine and vowed she would never stick her chewing gum
under the reception desk again.

Who else at the age of seventy could have love songs sung to her on
her birthday? If that's not unique enough, no other person I know would
be able to have a similar gathering of as many friends who were close and
caring in over four cities throughout this world. For those who snipe at
her heels we have one great message for them today and that is 'Sheila,
don't ever change' for we as friends acknowledge that her greatest
attribute is her vast capacity for loyalty to a friend. She has inspired and
comforted us. She has style and grace and beauty and has standards that
will not be compromised. She gives warmth, love and support to those
around her and our lives are enriched by this special friendship. Her loyalty and ferocious support for a friend are legend—there is no one I

would rather have on my side in a fight than Scotter. She has made a lasting contribution to all our lives and the proudest introduction we can make is: 'This is Sheila Scotter—my good friend Sheila Scotter.' In joy, Sheila, we acknowledge it is your seventieth birthday. In love and affection we thank you for your special friendship and support.

It was then my turn to say a few words—which I did with a certain amount of difficulty, as you can imagine. After my speech I went round to all the tables to thank everyone personally for an absolutely fabulous birthday party.

I should explain the reason it was held on 1 December. In 1990 the 2nd fell on a Sunday. The committee sensibly decided that a Saturday night was far more appropriate. As for that wretched tune I was worried about, I had never heard it rendered so brilliantly nor with such vigour as when the large dining room double doors opened and in marched an all-brass *jazz* band. No vocals, just 'Happy Birthday' booming out in a rhythm that made everyone get up on the dance floor immediately. I loved this band. I did not even resent them playing 'The old grey mare, she ain't what she used to be' when I cut the birthday cake! Again no vocals, but then everyone knew the words and had a good laugh.

As, in quoting Bill Haffenden's speech, I was not allowed to alter a single word (although my godson, he is also a barrister, so must be obeyed), I should perhaps clarify a couple of references he made. The first is his mention of 'Audrey' and that train trip. The full name of this character, played by the British actress Penelope Keith in a weekly television series, was Audrey Fforbes-Hamilton.

Secondly, when Bill mentioned 'an ill-informed journalist'

many loud 'hear! hear!'s were uttered in the ballroom. Most people had read a rather unkind interview with me, which had been published that morning in the Saturday *Age*. I have to blame myself for having been so silly as to agree to be interviewed by someone whom I did not know, for it started off with snide remarks that included 'her mellifluous voice and oh-so-proper enunciation'. I double-checked the meaning of 'mellifluous'. Did he really think my voice was flowing with honey when he obviously had a problem with words being pronounced clearly and distinctly? I found the whole article quite offensive, but what offended most was his degradation of my MBE. To quote the article: 'She received the MBE for services to journalism and commerce (is that an incongruous bracketing?). It may also seem odd that someone who has spent three decades offering handy fashion and household tips might win that elusive old MBE for excellence in journalism.' I did not quite understand what he meant by handy fashion hints and household tips over three decades. That MBE had been awarded in 1970 while I was a director of Condé Nast Publications and editor-in-chief of *Vogue* Australia and *Vogue Living* magazines, whose contributions to the fashion and homeware industries in this country had not gone unnoticed. Our whole team should have been recognised, I was the lucky one to receive the gong. I would have liked the offending journalist to have heard Bill Haffenden's speech that evening. He can, of course, read it now if he buys a copy of this book (*please* don't anyone *lend* him theirs!).

Concerning Bill's reference to the receptionist at his office: I thought then, and still think now, that it might have made more sense to say she made Roseanne look like Jackie Kennedy Onassis!

One can usually judge a party to have been a success if no one wants to leave. This was one of those memorable nights, wonderfully organised by others, when even I (normally a Cinderella-be-home-by-midnight-type) did not want it to end. *New Idea* covered the party with a double-page spread in their December issue the following week. I treasure my copy and, looking at it today, can truthfully say that most of my friends have not changed their looks in the intervening eight years ... but alas a few have changed their marital status.

---

I have already said how much I have enjoyed celebrating all my birthdays, but looking back it seems that every fifth year has been treated as a particularly important one.

At age sixty-five I was living in a converted stable in Millswyn Place, South Yarra, quite close to the Royal Botanic Gardens. My sixty-fifth party could be described as a '*déjeuner sur l'herbe*'. For readers who have seen Manet's famous 1863 painting in the Musée d'Orsay in Paris, or Picasso's 1962 linocut which he called 'luncheon on the grass (after Edouard Manet)', in the Australian National Gallery in Canberra, let me hasten to add that all the women at this particular picnic on the grass were fully clothed! Held on a Sunday (the day before my birthday), it was a BYO affair and about thirty of us brought scrumptious food in baskets or on platters and plenty of bottles of good wine to enjoy on the Oak Lawn in these marvellous gardens. The massive trees provided much-needed shade on this boiling-hot December day. We also had big round free-standing black and white umbrellas, which Douglas Butler had borrowed from Westpac. (That year, the bank was promoting a new product called Club 55. Each umbrella had a large red number 55 printed on it, to which Douglas had added an equally large 'PLUS 10'.) There were no speeches, but an English chum, James Dallmeyer, who was out here with AAP, had composed a rather flattering ode which he recited as a toast and then gave to me, handwritten inside a beautiful card. It read:

At the ripe old age of sixty-five
Those of us who are still alive
Begin to totter
Not she, not Sheila Scotter

All elegance in black and white
World citizen, now Yarra-ite
This daughter of the British Raj
is never ever not in charge

High priestess of Australian fashion
She reigned at Vogue with flair and passion
Some said that she was downright bossy
Despite insults, she got results
And left her mark on that fine glossy

Lest it be thought I am being churlish
Her other side is soft and girlish,
Warm and charming
Frank, disarming, full of wit
A girl still stacked with loads of 'IT'

Her beaux are famed
If seldom named
Some last for years, some only days
Before the parting of the ways

Usually for the heinous crime
Of staying after breakfast time

The more you know her the more you discover
A charity queen and a cricket lover
An author, columnist, opera buff
I could go on and on
But enough is enough

Among those worldwide who will toast her age
The odd former governor, designer Courrèges,
Balenciaga, Givenchy
Trent Nathan, Truscott and Royalty,
The mole of the species
And you and me
So raise your glass
A toast to class
To Sheila Scotter MBE.

On Monday the 2nd, John Truscott and I had a delicious cosy dinner with David and Fleur Gibbs at their home in South Yarra. At the time both David and I were on the Board of (what was then) the Victoria State Opera Company. I can assure you the conversation was not about age, as we all agreed with Groucho Marx that 'Age is not a particularly interesting subject. Anyone can get old. All you have to do is live long enough.' No, some very lively discussions on other matters took place.

Truscott, with his impeccable style and high professional standards, was pretty critical of the general manager of the VSO, then Kenneth Mackenzie-Forbes. Truscott thought that the VSO should be producing, to use his own words, 'little jewels of opera' that would match their budget rather than trying to compete with the full-time national Australian

Opera. He was adamant that, if policy was not changed, the company would eventually go broke. In hindsight, how right he was. Sadly, in October 1996 after some years of rather heavy losses, the Premier of Victoria, who was also Minister for the Arts, declined to bail them out again.

Going back a further five years, my sixtieth birthday was celebrated quietly over dinner à deux with Sir Robert Southey, one of my discreet (not dangerous) liaisons that year. He took me to La Madrague, one of his favourite restaurants, in South Melbourne. I hasten to add that this handsome charmer was a widower at the time and needless to say a very popular man about town. For several years now Bob has been married to Marigold (the late Sidney Myer's youngest daughter) and we are all friends ... *et je ne regrette rien.*

When I turned fifty-five I was living in London. I had to share my celebrations that year for, on the morning of 2 December 1975, my favourite cousin Bill Scotter (then a major general) was being knighted at Buckingham Palace. After his 'dubbing' by the Monarch, Bill had arranged for a Scotter family-and-friends lunch in the Army and Navy Club in Pall Mall. As my apartment was only a short walk from both the Palace and his club, I invited everyone to stop for a glass of bubbly on the way. It so happened that the legendary singer Vera Lynn was being made a Dame on the same day. So I asked her and her husband, and daughter Virginia Lewis, to come and join us for champagne. I was aware that Bill had admired her when she sang for the troops during World War II. What I had not known was that Dame Vera had another admirer: our dear old cockney porter who drove the tiny (French-type and jolly ancient) lift and took visitors personally to all the apartments at 73 St James's Street, always greeting them with 'Are you expected Sir (or Madame)?' before he let anyone in 'his' lift! Jack the porter, who was a keen collector of autographs, was absolutely ecstatic when Vera Lynn—now Dame Vera—gave him hers.

———————————

A letter from my mother for my fiftieth birthday:

*Oak Tree Cottage*
*Ringwood*
*Hampshire, UK*
*27 November 1970*

Darling Sheila
Can you really have reached your fiftieth birthday? It is very difficult to believe. And *what* you have achieved during those years!! More I suppose than the average octogenarian, and proud we are of you. Isn't it nice to feel we have tottered along sufficiently to be still here to congratulate you and wish you a very happy birthday, and lots more to come, as full of thrills and success as the first half.

Make yourself comfortable in your old age with that bedside table from us both and let us know the cost so that we can send you a cheque. Guy and Penny sent their presents off by sea about three weeks ago or earlier, so get the art book you are wanting from us for Xmas and again tell us how much. We'll be thinking of you and wishing you well. Have a lovely day.

Your letter came yesterday and your Vogue—a very good one this month.

I wonder if Guy and Penny told you they've bought a Labrador bitch puppy as a surprise for the children? A deep secret—to be called Sally Scotter.

Daddy and I went Christmas shopping yesterday in Bournemouth. It was just like spring! Rather tiring, the town was so packed with people.

Much love to you, dear, from Daddy and me, and our every good wish
Mummy

I still have that letter and treasure it, even though it was written all those years ago. I also have a carbon copy of my letter telling my parents about how I celebrated this particular birthday. It reads:

I had the most fabulous birthday, a really wonderful day. All my Vogue girls came to lunch in the apartment and I made a champagne punch. The cards I received were of course outstanding, especially now that I am NIFTY FIFTY! I still take the day off.

In the evening Sir Robert and Lady Chrichton Brown had about 100 people for cocktails and later on the Packers and Tony Larkins and I celebrated with dinner together. Frank P's birthday is at midnight (December 3rd). I had some super presents and yesterday your bedside-tray table arrived. Thank you both so very much. It will be an absolute joy to me, great for breakfast in bed and also for reading and writing, which I like doing sometimes from my bed.

You won't believe it but I too have done all my Christmas shopping except for you and Daddy. Am giving all my favourite chums large beach/garden umbrellas ... beautiful flowered ones, black with white flowers and navy with white flowers. Have found for individuals some superb little neck pillows with a tiny sunshade inside to keep the sun from one's face. I bought all these wholesale at fairly reasonable prices at one go. Other smaller presents ... the very best French cooking knives like the one you will see in Vogue in our December issue. One can never have too many knives in the kitchen and these are great. I am going to Tasmania for two days on December 17 and 18 and will be in Sydney for Christmas ... may go to Surfers Paradise for a few days between Christmas and New Year with the Packers who have an apartment up there. This is not absolutely definite ... but very probable.

All my love to you both darlings,
Sheila

I had not thought about writing any more about birthdays until I received an invitation to celebrate the Golden Jubilee of India's Independence on 15 August 1997.

The Honorary Consul for India and Mrs Vimala Rao were holding a large reception in Melbourne's Grand Hyatt Hotel. I privately wondered how many of their Australian guests had celebrated a very important birthday in their country well over fifty years before.

When I left school at seventeen, as my parents were not rich, I had the choice of either going to university in England or travelling in Europe before having what is termed a 'coming out season' in India. The choice was easy and made without hesitation; my passage to Bombay by sea was arranged. My parents were living in Alipore, Calcutta, and on my eighteenth birthday they generously gave me what was then termed 'a coming out ball' at the United Services Club.

Recalling what I wore then amuses me now. It was a fullskirted typically *'jeune fille'* ball gown, in pale turquoise silk taffeta, which had been designed for me by my Aunt Constance Gallay's couturier in Geneva. I wore it again at the Viceroy's ball at Government House in Belvedere where, although there were some beautiful gowns, no one outshone the splendour of the Indian princes and of their beautiful wives in ravishingly graceful colourful saris and magnificent jewels. I don't remember what happened to my dress but am pretty sure it sparked a vow that in future I would dress in black and white.

This eighteenth birthday was very important to me. Before it I had been allowed to go only to parties and dances that were chaperoned and given in private houses. But after it—in fact, the day after—my mother said to me, 'Sheila, now you can accept any invitations you wish, but do remember that in life you will be judged by the people with whom you are closely associated. So be careful darling.' I have never forgotten this advice. Come to think of it, it still governs my opinion of both men and women. Another piece of motherly advice to which I have definitely adhered was 'Never let your wants outstrip your needs.'

My other birthday present was a trip to Delhi, then on to Agra to see the fort and the magical Taj Mahal, and the ruins of the city of Fatephur Sikri. My father was then with Indian State Railways (Eastern Bengal) and we travelled in our own coach which, apart from its lack of airconditioning (this was early 1939), was quite luxurious. We were sort-of self-contained, as we had my father's bearer, a cook and one other servant with us, two bedrooms and a large-ish sitting–dining room. At night our coach used to be shunted off to a quiet siding, so we *needed* to be self-contained.

Back in Calcutta my life seemed to be an endless round of parties, as well as polo and cricket matches galore, which I adored watching. Daddy taught me to drive on the Maidan, a huge open park. He also coached me to improve my tennis (he was a very good player).

I learnt to fly an aeroplane ... but only in the air. My admirer of the moment was Oswold von Richthofen (nephew of the Red Baron) and he was the German Vice-Consul. It was his own plane that I was flying, so he would never let me land it, which annoyed me. Father was very anti-German and not at all pleased with this romance. 'Don't bring that Hun friend of yours back home,' he said. It was 1939 and Hitler was well on the way to declaring war. During the Blitz in London I often wondered whether Oswold was dropping some of the wretched bombs ... I knew he had joined the crack Hermann Goering squadron.

I was sad when it was time to take the boat train to Bombay and sail back to England in April 1939.

While I was happy, recently, to celebrate the fiftieth anniversary of the independence of the country of my birth,

I have to thank India and say how fortunate I was to experience such an unforgettable (now unrepeatable) start to an
adult life.

# 2

Merry Christmas to all my
friends—except two.

**W C Fields**

# Christmases to Remember

India was also host to the first four Christmases of my life. I was born in Calcutta, which is perhaps not the most glamourous of cities in that fascinating country. The climate in Bengal is uncomfortably humid and hot for part of the year and hotter still the rest. In those days (the early 1920s) the Viceroy always resided in Calcutta for Christmas.

At Government House in Belvedere there was traditionally a children's garden party at which Father Christmas arrived on an elephant. I was told by my parents that I was both frightened and impressed, but I do not remember these occasions.

I left India at four and went to boarding school in England from the age of four and a half to seventeen. These were happy years of my life. Boarding school suited my temperament: it gave me scope to be independent and to lead rather than follow (I have never been one to be pushed around).

When my parents were on leave from India we lived in the New Forest in Hampshire, which is where I spent most of my childhood. For readers not familiar with that area of England, it is between Southampton and Bournemouth and encompasses about 92,000 acres (or some 37,000 hectares) of breathtakingly beautiful woodlands, heather-clad moors, streams and riverlets. In typically English fashion the adjective 'New' has never been updated. It is, in fact, one of the oldest forests in the United Kingdom! During Saxon and Norman times it was the royal hunting ground. To this day people who live there still have grazing rights for their horses. Thinking of my Christmases in a thatched cottage in the New Forest brings back memories of huge log fires, carol singing (sometimes on our ponies, which was not easy but fun), church in the morning, traditional-roast-turkey-followed-by-Christmas-pud lunch, then listening to His Majesty the King (in my days George V) broadcasting his message to us on the wireless, and putting out plenty of crumbs for the robin redbreasts who, if there was a severe frost, added to the Christmas card look of our cottage. Our downstairs rooms were always filled with bunches of scarlet-berried holly from our own hedges. The tree was draped with the same comic old tinsel, silver stars and angels that were kept in boxes and brought out from year to year.

Christmas presents were opened after church. As children my two little brothers and I hung up pillowcases—not stockings—for Father Christmas to fill. We were fortunate kids with generous parents and relations but we had to obey a golden rule (a former old nanny's rule) and not use or play with any toy or game until we had written a thank-you letter to the giver. By chance or by persuasion one relation gave us writing paper every year. I confess, though, that this habit has obviously influenced me all my long life. Yes I still *write* thank-you notes—sometimes a little late, but eventually they are sent. Frankly I am appalled at how many children (adults, too) nowadays drag one to the telephone at a time that is convenient to *them* but can often be an interruption for you. One can't help thinking perhaps Fred Astaire was right when he said, 'The hardest job kids face today is learning good manners without seeing any.'

When my parents were not on leave from India (which was three years out of four) I used to spend school holidays either with grandparents in England or with cousins in Switzerland.

My paternal grandfather was, as they say, a 'man of the cloth' ... no, not a textile worker, nor a dress designer. Come to think of it, he often wore a frock—well, a surplice actually. He was Canon William Henry Scotter of Carlisle Cathedral in Cumberland. His parish was a small village called Witherslack. His ancient square-towered Norman church was opposite the vicarage next door to the village school. Witherslack was south of Cumberland, just over the border in Westmoreland—one of the most beautiful counties in the north of England, known to many as the Lake District.

Christmas time in this rambling stone vicarage (stone cold, too, from memory!) involved—inevitably—a lot of church-going plus carol singing with the village choir. I don't think my voice was appreciated much. I loved singing but I was no potential Joan Hammond; neither was the Witherslack choir exactly King's College material.

There had to be lots of giving before receiving, according to the Scriptures (and Canon Scotter), so we had to help with the village school's Christmas party before we had our own. We children (my brother Guy and other Scotter cousins; my youngest brother, Richard, was still in India) were allowed to help decorate Grandpa's quaint old church. While so doing, we were usually quite noisy and not always well-behaved, according to some rather prim regular voluntary 'flower ladies' who adored my grandfather. (I should explain he was a widower; my grandmother died when I was only four.) However, as there was no service taking place at the time, when anyone complained, the old boy would say, 'A church is a hospital for sinners, not a museum.' We loved him for that.

In my youth I spent quite a few holidays, including Christmases, with my cousins the Gallays in Geneva. I counted these as great treats—possibly because, compared with our fairly small cottage, their house in Bellevue seemed almost palatial. The garden was right on the edge of the lake, facing the highest mountain in the Alps, Mont Blanc.

Whereas I think that half of Switzerland (the Swiss–German half) tends to celebrate the feast of Saint Nicholas in early December, with the Gallays it was a totally English number … traditional turkey, ham, mince pies, rich cakes, crackers, and so on. My Aunt Constance was English, and Uncle Louis (her husband) was French–Swiss. Their children were a pretty good mixture and so was the language used between us. Frances, Ronald and Rosemary Gallay were tri-lingual: in French, German and English. I'm afraid I was lazy about speaking French in those days, but thankfully managed better later on in life, so perhaps it was not a bad start.

My Uncle Louis, whom I adored, was the first person to introduce me to what I used to describe as 'proper grown-up music'. I would go with him to concerts by the Suisse Romonde Orchestra whose resident conductor then was Ernst Ansermet. It was here that I first heard exciting new music played by an orchestra … the composer was Bartok.

At home my dear old father, even years later, would insist that Bartok sounded as if the orchestra were still tuning up.

During the 1970s, when I was living in London, I was privileged to share some rather special decorations at Christmas time. Let me explain. My apartment in 73 St James's Street was at the lower end near the post office and almost opposite St James's Palace. It was also only a stone's throw from where Her Majesty the Queen Mother lives (well, not *my* kind of throw, more like one by Glenn McGrath).

About ten days before 25 December, miniature Christmas trees covered with tiny bud lights were placed on the broad ground-floor outside windowsills of Clarence House. The Queen Mother (bless her) wanted everyone to enjoy them, I was told by my then neighbour Lord Maclean, a delightful Scot known to friends as Chips Maclean. As he was the Lord Chamberlain, he and his wife resided in St James's Palace right on the corner where Pall Mall turns into St James's. Their sitting room was on the first floor. It had an uncurtained bow window in which they always displayed an enchanting silvery-white tree covered with silver and gold lights. Their idea, too, was to share with passers-by—and of course we locals passed by more than most.

Another big tradition in the build-up to Christmas in London was the placing of an immense pine tree in Trafalgar Square. About sixty feet (eighteen metres) high and illuminated with literally hundreds of coloured lights, an identical tree has been donated by Norway every year since 1945 as a 'thank you' to the people of England for what they did in World War II. To be politically correct, I should say to the people of the *United Kingdom*, not just England. I hope I do not offend anyone but I am reminded of Oscar Wilde who once said, 'The Scots keep the Sabbath and anything else they can lay their hands on. The Welsh pray on their knees and their neighbours. The Irish will fight for anything and not know what they are fighting for. The Englishman is a selfmade man, thus relieving the Almighty of a grievous responsibility.'

During my six and a half years as a resident of London, I spent three Christmases with my friend Florence Packer (widow of Sir Frank Packer—also once a close friend, but that's another story ...). Florence lives in Monaco, the tiny principality at the foot of the southern alps on the Mediterranean coast, not far from the French–Italian border. I adored staying in her rather super apartment high up overlooking the whole of Monte Carlo. Her petite and fascinating Russian mother, Masha Porges, who was alive then, always hosted a Christmas lunch for about ten friends at the Hôtel de Paris. Neither she nor Florence ever cooked, not even to boil an egg, yet both were connoisseurs of good food.

I recall Florence not being too impressed with the hotel's attempt at traditional plum pudding—or rather, the sauce served with it. This was more like custard with a shot of liqueur in it and was called 'sauce anglais', which to me seemed a bit insulting. Lady P, who has what is known as a 'sweet tooth', loved proper brandy butter (called 'hard sauce' by some). 'Sheila, you know how to make it,' she said on my second visit. 'Let's take our own this year.' We did. I made it the night before, and left it to harden in the refrigerator in two empty cashew nut tins that were going to be easy to carry.

I shall never forget the look on the face of the head waiter of one of Europe's poshest hotels when he was handed these two garish bright blue tins with golden nuts painted on the outside. 'For Madame Porges' table?' he queried, as if he was receiving poison for the Prince de Polignac who was already seated with Masha. When the ever generous Florence gave him a tip he eventually smiled and agreed to have the contents of our ghastly tins put into something worthy of a French aristocrat.

In Monte Carlo most people send and receive flowers and plants at Christmas time. Popular Lady P received pots and pots of bright red poinsettias and deep red azaleas all trimmed with red satin bows. We took off the bows and pinned these to the dark green ivy covered balustrade on the balcony ... no need for other decorations in this apartment.

My recipe for brandy butter is based entirely on Robert Carrier's recipe in *Robert Carrier's Cookery Course*. I confess that occasionally I substitute some icing sugar but really think he is right in calling for all castor sugar, as this gives it the slightly crunchy texture. For four people, you need 115g unsalted butter, 115g castor sugar and 2 tablespoons of good brandy. To prepare, soften the butter with a wooden spoon, then beat it until smooth and fluffy. (Yes, this is hard work but, I find, produces a much better result than using a blender.) Put aside a level tablespoon of castor sugar and add the remainder to the creamed butter. Do this gradually, beating vigorously until the mixture is very fluffy and almost white. Now soak the remaining sugar in brandy and incorporate it into your butter cream, just a little at a time, and beat until smooth again. Chill until firm. I often use more brandy but one must be careful not to let the mixture get too liquidy or too soft. It has to be hard when scooped onto a slice of hot pudding. It is simply scrumptious with cold pud, too.

I once cooked an English-type Christmas lunch for Rex Harrison. This was in 1984 while he was in Australia acting with Claudette Colbert in the classic Somerset Maugham play 'Aren't We All?'. After opening in Melbourne, the play toured Brisbane before going to Perth on 27 December. Instead of spending Christmas in Queensland then flying direct to Western Australia, Rex wanted to come back to Melbourne, and asked if they (he and his sixth wife) could have Christmas lunch with me in South Yarra, where I was living at the time. During the run of the play he had lunched there two or three times while his wife was in Hong Kong and he always wanted shepherd's pie and bread-and-butter pudding. We both agreed, I remember, with Elizabeth Ray, the highly respected culinary expert, who once said, 'I have always maintained that there is nothing wrong with nursery food now that we are grown up and can have a glass of wine with it.'

For Christmas Rex wanted the full traditional menu: roast turkey with all the trimmings ... chipolata sausages, bread sauce, baked potatoes, rich gravy and 'Could the vegetables include brussels sprouts?' Goodness knows where I found them at that time of the year, but Rex adored them, so they were compulsory. When I say I cooked this particular lunch, I have to confess that I am not reticent about asking for help from close friends who are good cooks. Douglas Butler took care of the plum pudding and brought it just to re-heat. (Of course I had made proper brandy butter.) John Stanistreet not only stuffed and tied up the legs of the huge turkey the night before, but also brought a dish of glazed carrots (he is a whiz at these).

Douglas Butler and I had taken the Harrisons to the Christmas Eve Carols by Candlelight service in the Sidney Myer Music Bowl. Fortunately we had reserved seats but we had to walk through a crowd of thousands of people to get to them. Every now and then we heard some applause and remarks like 'Isn't that Sexy Rexy?' When told he was recognised, instead of shuffling along with me, Harrison drew himself up to his full height and entered like the star he was.

During his three months in Melbourne I had grown to rather like the old chap. I suppose I was fortunate to meet him in his more mellow days, as I had heard from people who had known him for years how jolly cranky and difficult he could be. We did, however, have one thing in common: a love of cricket. On Boxing Day I invited him to the 8am Lord's Taverners pre-Test match breakfast as guest of honour. In 1984 Rex Harrison was seventy-nine and not at all keen on starting his day early. Being on the Victorian Committee that organises this important fundraising breakfast, I was somewhat concerned. I need not have worried. The old darling was a serious cricket lover (and I gather not a bad player in his youth), and he turned up punctually at the Hilton on the Park. When he was introduced to draw the raffle prizes he was utterly charming to everyone and received a standing ovation.

This Boxing Day was one of Melbourne's coolest of summer days. Rex was well wrapped up—a short overcoat, a scarf, plus his famous 'Henry Higgins' hat—when we walked across to the Melbourne Cricket Ground at 10.45am.

We were playing the Poms and it turned out to be a disastrous day for Australia, who lost five wickets before the luncheon interval. The only smiling face in the committee box that morning was Harrison's. Before we went in for drinks and lunch, Rex and I hung our hats on pegs at the entrance to the dining room. I remember being asked by Rosemary Lill (who, with her husband Dr John Lill, general manager of the MCG, was a good chum of mine) whether I would mind taking *my* hat off the peg. Golly, I thought, I've obviously made a ghastly boo-boo and broken a golden rule about non-members' hats in this holy of holies. No such thing, thank goodness. Dear Rosie only wished to hang *her* hat alongside RH's Henry Higgins number and take a photograph!

With the aid of his binoculars (he had very bad eyesight) Rex hardly took his eye off the ball during the whole day, not even when he was in the 'loo. Inevitably he was sceptical when I told him that he would still be facing the wicket right behind the bowler's arm. 'You are quite right,' he said when he came back to his seat. 'But how the hell did you get in there to find out?' No comment.

For anyone in my age group who is single and whose immediate family relations live on the other side of the world, Christmas holiday time in Australia can be quite lonely. But during my years here, Sagittarian luck has held. Generous and much loved friends have invited me to their homes, some of which are the most beautiful in the southern hemisphere, where I have been pampered and spoilt. Out of respect for these friends' privacy, I won't go into details here. Suffice to say that some of my happiest Christmases have been those spent with Kerry and Ros Packer at their beach house in New South Wales (I am godmother to their daughter Gretel Barham), and with my dearest friend Margaret Darling on her magnificent property at Woomargama, also in New South Wales.

Being a Christmas guest of Robert Carrier—one of my favourite men—is also quite a treat. In England once we had a Christmas breakfast (actually nearer the lunch hour) cooked by RC himself. It was when he owned Hintlesham Hall, a heavenly Queen Anne house in Suffolk. That night we had Christmas dinner nearby in a sweet old house called 'Christmas Cottage', which belonged to our mutual friend and former editor of British *Vogue*, Ailsa Garland.

I have also enjoyed a few Christmases with my oldest chums Vernon and Shirley Churchill-Simmonds in the heart of the New Forest in Hampshire. Since my parents died in 1977 Vernon and Shirley lovingly tell me that I am to regard their Manor Farm, Burley, as my second home.

One Christmas several decades ago was rather different for me. In 1973, having spent most of that year enjoying myself in England, I decided it was time I did something for other people at this special time of the year. There is a char- ity in London called 'Crisis at Christmas'. I first heard of it through the British actor Ronnie Corbett, who was on their Board of Trustees. During the period of 22 to 27 December this charity provides 'open house' for homeless or destitute London people in need of food and companionship. To be homeless is tragic; to be homeless and alone doubly so. For these unfortunate people, of course, the crisis lasts all year round, but thank goodness there are many hostels who nor- mally take care of them. Alas, these are obliged to close to enable their hardworking staff to spend Christmas with their own families. In 1973 the Archbishop of Canterbury had made available an empty old church, the Church of St Mary, near Lambeth Palace on the south side of the River Thames.

Volunteer helpers were allocated shifts. Mine was from 11.30am to 1.30pm. I walked from my apartment across St James's Park, past the Houses of Parliament and across Lambeth Bridge. It was a longish lonely walk—in fact, I hardly saw a soul as obviously most people would have been preparing lunch. I reported for duty at 11.15am, believing that one should always be at least fifteen minutes early when relieving anyone from a shift so that they are not worried whether you are coming or not. In situations like this helpers can hardly leave until they are replaced. My job was mainly to serve the meals, and to help out in the kitchen when wanted. Doling out the food was very rewarding and it kept me reasonably warm. (The weather was bitterly cold and, as all our cooking was done on petrol/gas stoves, no doors were permitted to be closed.)

To my horror, when I arrived on Boxing Day, I was told I was to be in charge of the kitchen, as the head cook was sick. The main meal was to be a fricassee-cum-stew made from leftover turkey. Sounds all right, I thought ... but it was for three hundred people! My part-time course at the Cordon Bleu School of Cookery (which I was attending that year) was of no help here. We had to cook in huge cauldrons, which meant using kilos (not grams) of flour *in each* to make a tasty sauce. Chicken and turkey stock had been donated by Crosse & Blackwell in large cans. Likewise, kilos and kilos of butter (from memory, Australian) had been given to us. This bloomin' turkey stew must have been acceptable in the end because some of the other volunteer helpers asked if they could have some, too.

Mind you, had I known beforehand that I had to cook

it, I would have adapted Robert Carrier's recipe for curried leftover turkey. From his book *Entertaining*, a favourite of mine, his recipe is to sauté, in four tablespoons of butter, one finely chopped Spanish onion and two thinly sliced stalks of celery until the onion is transparent. You then add one peeled, cored and diced apple, a finely chopped clove of garlic and a tablespoon *each* of curry powder and flour (having mixed them together). Continue to cook, stirring constantly, until the mixture begins to turn golden. Now add 425ml of chicken stock and cook the sauce, stirring again until it is smooth and thick. Then add 680g of cooked turkey and a tablespoon of finely chopped parsley. Carrier suggests serving the curried turkey in a ring of cooked rice. I have done this but I do not think it would have been easy to serve it this way in the Church of St Mary.

---

Readers may have gathered by now that I am a very organised person, and keep a comprehensive filing system. Sorting through my bulky Christmas file I found a page from the *Sunday Observer* dated 22 December 1985. The paper no longer exists in Victoria but at the time Roland Rocchiccioli was their Sunday Man About Town reporting on Melbourne's social scene. He had asked some 'well-known personalities' what they wanted and what they did not want for Christmas that year. About me, he wrote that 'the elegant black-and-white Sheila Scotter would love to be given a chauffeur-driven car to be at her disposal every day, a bunch of white daisies every week, and a case of French champagne every month. ' "What I could well do without," she explained, "is a one-way ticket to South Africa, an airmail subscription to *Pravda*, and a copy of Ita Buttrose's book on etiquette." ' I had to remind myself that this was said in 1985—some thirteen years ago. I would still love to be chauffeur-driven, and as apartheid has ended I would quite like to visit South Africa, especially if I could meet Nelson Mandela. As for white flowers, yes, I would love a bunch every week and I would never refuse champagne but would be very happy with a case of good Australian wine each month!

This Christmas file used to hold lengthy lists of cards received, with dates and senders' names, plus cards sent and to whom. I used to mail between three and four hundred a year in those days. The postage was considerably less than today; likewise the cost of the cards. Now, I limit the list to family and favourite friends overseas, and people who are sick or lonely, and that is about it. But oh dear, the feeling of guilt every time I receive greetings from anyone who has taken the trouble to remember me. I partly solve this 'feeling-guilty-and-slightly-mean' problem by thanking people during the month of January. This was made easier in 1996 when, at my local post office, I came across packets of 'Official Last Minute Christmas Cards' (reduced in price!) by the Ink Group of Alexandria, New South Wales. Apart from 'Merry Christmas and Happy New Year', each included a short paragraph that said 'This card conforms to all official guidelines pertaining to belated wishes and is as sincere as any card you may have received on time.' Believe me, I mailed quite a few! I now keep some in my desk drawer alongside a small supply of 'Sorry I forgot your birthday' cards.

Isn't it curious that so many retailers promise that 'This Christmas will be the greatest ever!' ... I always thought the first one was.

**3**

It's no use saying we are doing our best.
You have got to succeed in doing what is necessary.

**Winston Churchill**

# n Fashion

I must acknowledge that I owe my career in fashion to Australia—or rather to one remarkable Australian woman who persuaded me to leave London for an exciting job in Melbourne. We met when I was working at Spectator Sports Ltd, a member of the London Model House group, owned by the designer known simply as Wallace.

After the war, I was determined to make my career in fashion but, apart from a love of beautiful clothes (even as a child), I had no idea how to go about it and no qualifications other than a reasonably good figure.

One day at lunch with chums I met a top executive with Spectator Sports who suggested 'Come and model for us. Start at the bottom and if you are serious you can learn the whole business.' I was. And I did.

Instead of sitting in the model room when not showing the collection, I used to make a nuisance of myself in the packing department, checking how everything was distributed to retailers, and seeing how production costs were arrived at, how fabrics were purchased, how different buyers placed orders, and so on. After a few months I was promoted: I was put in charge of the showroom and of presenting the collections to retail store buyers from all over the world.

In August 1948 we received an unexpected call from the London office of the Myer Emporium, Melbourne, to say that Miss Doris McFadyen, who bought all their imported fashion, had just arrived in the UK from Australia and wished to see our range. I had never heard of the Myer Emporium, so quickly checked on the last few years' orders and realised this was an important buyer.

What worried me was that, at this off-season quiet time of the year, both our permanent models were on leave. I explained to Miss McFadyen that the clothes she would be seeing had originally been made on me and that I would be happy to model for her if she did not mind a slow presentation. She preferred it, she said, and before leaving she placed a very large order.

Doris McFadyen returned to London in September and again bought heavily from our new collection. She did not like flying, so came by sea and stayed two months in Europe. Once or twice during her stay, we had lunch together and discussed my career.

'What about coming to Australia to work with Myer?' she asked me.

'What kind of job would it be?' I questioned and almost fainted when she said 'To replace me in about a year's time.'

I was twenty-seven years old and assumed I would perhaps be an assistant buyer for some time before getting a job like this. If Myer had been in the United States I would not have hesitated, but Australia was not exactly on my list, so I asked for time to think it over.

We had more lunches and before Miss McFadyen left she said, 'Look Sheila, we are having a very big Norman

Hartnell fashion show prior to the Royal visit [George VI and Queen Elizabeth] next year. Hartnell is bringing out his famous top model, Dolores, and we want one other from England. Why not you?'

I explained I did not want to go 'backwards' and arrive just as a model. 'But this way you will have a return air ticket and can come and see the place.' Doris McFadyen was a very persuasive woman and I trusted her. So I agreed. My family was not *against* it; my father merely said, 'I doubt if you will want to live there, but go for it.'

The arrangement was that Norman Myer, the managing director, who was due in London soon, would interview me and make it official. But his visit was cancelled for some reason and I was asked, through the London office of Myer, to hold on to my present job for a few more weeks as Bill Ricker, the merchandising director, was coming over. In hindsight I think this was good old Sagittarian luck. Ricker was a tough, straight-from-the-shoulder sort of bloke and when I was appointed by him people automatically thought I must be good at my job. He was also a happily married family man and wonderful to work for. In fact, I should thank him as well as Doris McFadyen.

As it happened, King George became ill and Hartnell's visit was cancelled; no point in showing gorgeous ball gowns when there were no Royal Balls. So the return trip by air was no longer necessary, and in April 1949 I set sail for Melbourne aboard the Orient liner *Orcades*. Myer had found me a flat in Adams Street, South Yarra (hideous furniture but a jolly nice flat).

I simply adored working for Doris McFadyen. We had

the same sense of humour and the same taste in fashion, and she taught me how to sell expensive clothes to women who could sometimes be quite difficult to please—the knack of giving guidance with absolute authority. Like me, Doris did not respect rank ... even Norman Myer was slightly scared of her.

You can imagine that this was a challenging time for me. Here I was, at only twenty-eight (from memory the youngest buyer in the store), going to inherit Doris's job (her husband had made her promise to retire at fifty-two), with the two top saleswomen, Miss Cody and Miss Brew being in their fifties. I needed these women on side, as they accounted for most of the sales figures from their lists of regular fashionable clients.

In those days the Model Salon, as it was named, sold only imported clothes—which made it influential and important within the store itself. Whenever I came back from an overseas buying trip I gave a visual report on the latest colours, fabrics, cuts and so on for other departments. The basic fashion industry made quite good quality clothes but they relied mainly on copies from continental magazines in those days (early 1950s). I was, I recall, popular with the shoe department buyers (all young men whom I liked) as I would show them all the fashion colours. This meant that we would never lose a sale because the customer could not find the right pair of shoes; suitable choices were even brought up to the salon if necessary. No wonder these men's names— Steele, Rosenhain, Glowery, Hayden and Schattner—ended up in the top ranks of Myer management.

Oh dear, I wish this book had been written by someone else. While this may sound odd to you, dear reader, it seems very clear to me that it would be so much easier to write a biography than an autobiography.

The rest of my career in the fashion world was summed up accurately on 19 June 1962 by Condé Nast Australia in a press release announcing my appointment as editor of *Vogue* Australia and *Vogue* New Zealand. I am not exactly the blushing type, but when I found it recently in one of my files, I thought, 'Gosh, how did I manage to do all that?' Of course a press release is hardly likely to make *un*flattering comments, but in the main the facts are right ... so I quote:

Miss Sheila Scotter has been appointed Editor of the Australian and New Zealand editions of *Vogue,* and will be taking up her appointment in Sydney at the beginning of October. Miss Scotter, a woman of tremendous vitality and enthusiasm, is an internationally recognised authority in the fields of fashion and textiles.

For the past four years she has been handling one of the most coveted promotional positions in the world—Directrice of the promotion activities of the Banlon and Everglaze trademarks for Continental Europe, with headquarters in Paris. This job has given her entrée to all the Paris Couture houses—she speaks French fluently—and today many designers are her personal friends.

Over the four years she has been continuously meeting the top people, not only in Paris, but in all the international fashion and textile centres—New York, London, Zurich, Geneva, Milan, Rome, Florence, Mulhouse—and her impact on the cotton industry in Europe has been immense. Her advice on design, new production and selling plans was constantly sought. This first-hand knowledge of the world's textile and fashion markets will be an invaluable contribution, not only to *Vogue* Australia, but to the progress of the whole Australian fashion industry.

Miss Scotter's ambition has been to work from the ground up. She started as a model in London with the house of Frederick Starke, and has worked through all facets of the fashion world—wholesale, retail buying and selling, advertising and promotion—a career which is culminating now in what she terms 'the fascinating fulfilment of being chosen as Editor of the two youngest members of the Vogue family'.

Miss Scotter's great love for Australia started when she was brought out here in 1949 by the Myer Emporium. After four years as buyer for their Imported Model Showroom, she went to Georges Limited as high-fashion co-ordinator and buyer for their model clothes, furs and the boutique. In 1956 she launched the Everglaze Marketing Division for Joseph Bancroft & Sons of Wilmington, Delaware, USA in Australia and New Zealand, and made an outstanding success. It was a great honour to be chosen for their top post in Paris, a position strongly competed for by both European and American personnel.

While in Paris she never lost touch with Australia. Her office was a constant meeting place for many Australians visiting the centre of fashion. She has the ability to discover new talent in designers, artists and photographers, and many of the people she has encouraged are world famous today.

The last paragraph announced my plan to spend the next four months in the Paris, London and New York offices of Vogue, to familiarise myself with the publications' international editorial policies. I would also cover the Paris winter couture collections on behalf of *Vogue* Australia.

And so I began, some three decades ago, what was to become the most challenging and exciting period of my career in fashion.

---

In my early days at Vogue I realised that we had to make it easy for people with talent to come and talk to us: young photographers, young writers, artists of all kinds, aspiring but shy models, plus of course young designers (even old designers, for that matter). For some, just to enter the offices of *Vogue* magazine is nerve-racking, and I did not want a receptionist to say, 'Have you an appointment? ... You know the editor is a very busy woman' (which I did overhear one day). So I explained that, if anyone wanted to see someone from editorial, one of us would come out to meet them, look quickly at what they wanted to show us, and make a time that suited them to come back and have a proper meeting in my office. If we were free, of course, we would do this straight away.

But I never forget a tip from Carmel Snow, editor of (the US) *Harper's Bazaar* and one of the most revered and influental figures in her time. She was the first to publish Truman Capote. He arrived with no appointment and the receptionist at Bazaar, who knew Carmel Snow's policy of always seeing people herself, was diffident this time. 'He looks most peculiar, very shy, and has brought in a short story,' she told the boss. Carmel met Capote, and liked the story and published it. After that, *anything* that he wrote was shown to *Harper's Bazaar* first.

I vowed to myself that *Vogue* Australia would foster

budding talent and I wanted it known that our door was always open.

During my *Vogue* days (and please remember I am looking back some thirty years) we were fortunate that there was virtually no competition from other glossy magazines. Ironically our biggest competitors were other Condé Nast *Vogues*—American, British and French—but in those days these arrived by surface mail weeks late and contained only foreign merchandise.

Apart from Elizabeth Reeve, my associate editor, and myself (both over forty), the editorial team were all very young, but full of creative talent, jolly hard workers for low pay, and just as enthusiastic as I was to show the Vogue flag and raise the standard of the entire fashion scene. Editorially our job was to lead, to inform, and to guide the (then) pretty unsophisticated fashion industry.

Outside office hours, Condé Nast Australia's managing director Bernard Leser and I agreed that it was important to provide constructive criticism of the industry. So I did frequent radio, press and television interviews. We were particularly worried about lack of co-operation between fabric manufacturers and designers of clothing. I well recall the first time I 'sat in' on a fashion 'run-through' given by Diana Vreeland (known as 'DV') when she was editor of American *Vogue*. 'Now listen to me, *fabric makes fashion*,' she told her fashion and accessory editors. 'And this means it starts in Margaret Ingersoll's office.' Margaret had always been a highly respected fabric editor but rose to great importance during DV's days. From then on, during my visits to the New York office, I *always* spent time with Ingersoll in her treasure trove of exciting new fabric swatches before I did anything else.

Not surprisingly, I quickly became somewhat critical of the lack of importance of textiles in relation to fashion in this country, but Sir Robert Webster, Chairman of the Textile Council of Australia, may not have been aware of my views when he asked me whether I would speak at their first Australian Textile Congress in Canberra. I thought 'what a great opportunity', especially as he said 'Choose your own subject, but speak frankly.' My address, given on 27 September 1965, was entitled 'The Importance of Fashion in Relation to Textiles'.

I cannot state my views any more clearly now than I did then; but the speech I gave was rather long, so I hope that readers will forgive me if, by way of sharing my thoughts with you, I partly paraphrase and partly quote.

I began with the fundamental point that fashion, with its implications and repercussions, is the catalyst that makes the textile industry move. Changing fashion and changing tastes were then, and are still, the two major forces that make the buying public fed up with what they've got. I have often been asked 'What is fashion?' I've tried to define it in one sentence, a sentence that represents the way *I* feel about it: in the final analysis all women's fashion is an expression of contemporary thought and taste in the form of women's clothes. Perhaps the important word is *contemporary*.

My next point was directed specifically at the textiles industry of the 1960s:

Fashion has long since ceased to be of interest only to the rich—thanks to the stupendous job done by your industry, the fabric houses, the makers-up and their use of fabrics, by the producers of paper patterns, by the stores, and I would add by magazines and newspapers. Fashion is read about and followed by women of every age and in every income group. Fashion nowadays is completely international, and all over the world there are people who feel fashion trends and who express them in completely original forms. Nevertheless, without belittling the contributions made by designers in other countries, it must be agreed that Paris is still the great international fashion centre. Twice a year, at the time of the couture openings, buyers, journalists and endless other people concerned with the fashion trade pour into Paris from all over the world. They come not only to see the clothes created by the great couturiers, but to study all the ingredients that go to make those clothes—the fabrics, the accessories, the buttons, the trimming and the colours.

It is, of course, an over-simplification of a very complex subject to say that fashion is born in Paris, but it is certainly true to say that many ideas that have previously been floating about in the air take their first concrete form as clothes on the runways of the great houses. Some, having got so far, still never become fashion as we know it today. Because, unless a line is accepted by the international experts, imported by them and reproduced on the spot in a form acceptable to their particular part of the world, it does not really make an impact and become an accepted fashion.

I felt that those basic remarks regarding the importance of the Paris influence on *all* aspects of fashion needed to be said. Among the hundreds of textile tycoons and executives in the audience, I was positive that only a very small percentage would be aware of it. Today, of course, many visit France regularly, before their trips to New York or Milan.

Next, I wanted to address the tremendously important

issue of colour in fashion. I introduced the subject by quoting
Cecil Beaton:

'Perhaps no element making the total fashion image is as important
as colour.' It is colour that inspires and vitalises the new as well as the old
in fabric today. Colour needs, therefore, a lot of deep thought and more
study than ever before. There was a happy time years ago when one could
fairly safely bet that the colours shown in strength in Paris one season
would be in strength in the bulk market the same season the following
year. Not so now. It can, and very often does, happen that Paris couture
and the important ready-to-wear markets show largely the same colours
almost at the same time. But Paris (and in their summer collections, Italy)
can afford to be adventurous and put in unexpected colours ... maybe one
model here, one there. These are, for the want of a better word, what I call
'creepers'. Sometimes one sees them creeping for several seasons before
they are due to burst into full bloom. Other times because they are creeping in lots of collections you know they are already on their way and will
become a new fashion colour very quickly.

I expressed my belief that colour in fashion is not only a
matter of *a* colour, but of a *type* of colour. In my early days as
editor of *Vogue* a very great French designer said to me that, in
his opinion, it was just as easy to look dowdy in a bright colour
when fashion called for muted shades as the other way round.
I must say I have seen him proved right over and over again. In
a very important way fashion also governs the construction of
fabrics and types of fabrics. Fabrics must depend to a large
extent on the fashion line. When it is casual and loose, soft
materials take precedence; when it becomes more tailored,
firmer fabrics are to the fore. The really successful colourist

must also be conscious of changing and developing lines.

What I wanted to put over to my audience was that fashion in its contemporary sense had ceased to be *seasonal*. I explained:

Right now the look and line governing and influencing everyone, both in the United States and Europe, is the line of André Courrèges. To illustrate the force of his influence, Courrèges did *not* present a collection in Paris this August. But did anyone take his place? No. On the contrary. I saw the leading haute couture collections myself last month and I assure you, many a Courrèges-inspired dress, suit and coat popped up and everyone (with the exception of Givenchy but including the master Balenciaga) was influenced enough to shorten their skirt lengths to knee length or just above. Perhaps the last comparable fashion impact made by one single designer was in 1947 when Christian Dior brought skirts down and produced what was then called the 'New Look'.

Getting back to Courrèges, he seems to have produced not only clothes that are wanted by women, but also clothes that even rival designers recognise are wanted by today's women. His philosophy is uncluttered simplicity, comfortable and easy-to-wear fashion, and my goodness this accent on line gives the fabric industry a fabulous opportunity to exploit. If at any time one can say that fine fabrics make fine fashion, it is now.

I then gave a short critical assessment of the 1960s textile industry as I saw it. In my (then) sixteen years in fashion, I had worked seven purely in textiles—three years in Australia and just over four in Europe. I had studied the fashion-making textile industry, worked closely with them and (hoping not to sound too immodest) sometimes inspired the people

concerned ... and some of them had been French! So I felt qualified to praise the Australian textile industry.

Today there is no question of people saying 'Oh well, we can't get
that in Australia.' With the exception of certain experimental yarns, we
can. And we have a fabulous industry that could make anything. But
does the general public, whose interests we are in business to serve, fully
realise this? I do not believe they do. I hate to say this but there are too
many women who still think that, because a fabric is from Italy or
France, it automatically represents better taste and fashion than an
Australian fabric. A great deal of effort goes into awards for this and
that, and the *trade* is aware of these efforts. But surely the battle is
really to get any outstanding and new ideas across to the public and
accepted by them.

Our great loss is that so many of our outstanding creative efforts in
the textile field never finish up where the public have the opportunity to
buy them easily. [...] So many pipelines from producer to consumer
become clogged somewhere along the line. Of course it is always easier to
make a whipping boy out of the retail buyer. We all know there are many
outstanding buyers in this country, but in my opinion there are numerous
people with the *title* 'fashion buyer' who have no intention of actually
buying *fashion*, and some who don't even know the meaning of fashion
and certainly don't follow it. There is the general tendency to play safe.
This means too many worthwhile fashion ideas (worthwhile at least in the
sense that they ought to be tried out) are still-born.

Wishing to stay alive a little longer, I declined to elaborate. What I *did* risk saying was that, here in Australia, we
had several priceless assets:

we do have a discerning buying public with taste and fashion sense. And these women buy on colour and styling first, on quality second, and on price third … *not* the other way round. We also have a whole school of young creative designers who, with their individuality, their dedication, their push, their enthusiasm, talent and ability, are of world standard. I really believe that it is our responsibility to promote and foster this Australian talent to the maximum, and continue to do so because—long term—it is the best way to serve our industry as a whole. These designers cannot work without textiles and we notice they import a lot to get what they want.

I knew what I was talking about; I had interviewed one of them and had been told that when he started he was forced to go overseas to firms to get co-operation re colouring … His colours? Fashion colours. No one here would colour specially for him. They would sell him only *their* colours. Two overseas converters, however, not only produced his special colour selection but eventually incorporated it into their own ranges. Gradually he became established, his collections selling well, and was more in demand every season. As I spoke, one Australian mill that was working with him on the basis that he wanted had a firm order for 700 pieces for the coming winter season (approximately 31,000 metres). It was not a bad order! And this designer was growing in both importance and volume. Again, at the beginning, the same thing had applied to prints. Naturally his first orders were smaller, but now his *minimum* first order with a printer for one design was 4570 metres. By the way, the printer/converter who once would not do business with this designer was now begging him to colour and style for them. This change of attitude in three short years.

I challenged all sales managers in the textile industry to

**Above left:** First steps at 14 months and my first almost knee-length dress. My uncle, Stanley Bazeley, is behind me. **Above right:** My brother Guy and I on one of our daily early morning walks with our *Ayah* in Calcutta, 1924. **Below left:** Aged four and showing my knickers, but only on the balcony at home in Calcutta. **Below right:** In my fairy costume and dancing shoes. I should explain that we children were photographed every holiday for our parents in India. This shot was taken by a devoted grandmother Emma Bazeley.

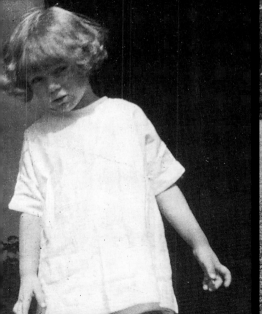

**Above top:** In my Bazeley grandparents' garden with a new hairstyle. **Above:** Guy Scotter and I (centre), with our Swiss cousins Francis and Ronald Gallay (left and right). **Below:** Hoping my little legs will control that fat pony Nimrod at my prep school Lordswood House, Hampshire, UK.

Above left: My youngest brother, Richard Scotter, aged 18 months. Above right: With my favourite teddy bear and my cousin Francis Gallay. Am relieved to realise that my legs improved with age. Below left: Aged 7, with my beloved grandfather, the Reverend (later Canon) William Henry Scotter, in his vicarage at Witherslack, Westmoreland, UK. Below right: Guy and I, with my mother Winifred Alice Scotter on leave in England, June 1929.

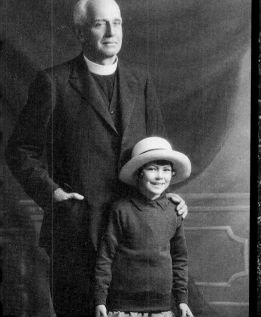

**Above left:** With my first husband Geoffrey Batten-Pearce on the steps of St Peter's Church, Vere Street, Mayfair, London, 19 December 1942. **Above right:** On our honeymoon, skiing in Zermatt. (The war was still on but Switzerland was neutral!) **Below left:** During my courtship with Alan Ford McIntyre, snapped by Elspeth Juda of the *Ambassador* magazine (UK) as she was leaving for London from Essendon Airport in 1951. **Below right:** A favourite photo of my second husband. We were married in Melbourne on 11 September 1951 when I was 31.

**Above:** My parents Harold Gordon Scotter and Winifred Alice Scotter attending a wedding in Brockenhurst, New Forest, UK. **Below:** My brother Guy Scotter at Larkhill on Salisbury Plain when he was a captain in the Royal Artillery, with his labrador retriever.

Above left: I wonder why Sir Robert Southey looks so amused. Was I whispering something or just enjoying hugging him? Above right: With Harold Holt on Dunk Island. Zara Holt once told me she was aware of her husband's many liaisons. She knew that I had more than flirted with him. I knew she knew, and we still remained friends. Below left: Claude Alcorso and I on a beach in Tasmania. Below right: With Sydney photographer Robert Rosen. And two much loved close friends, the late Sir Brian Murray (left) and the late Sir Anthony Griffin. I envy the angels.

Oh, innocent victims of Cupid, remember this terse little verse. To let a fool kiss you is stupid. To let a kiss fool you is worse. (E Y Harburg)

**Above left:** When Ted and Heather Lustig were married the reception was at the Grand Hyatt Melbourne (where else?). Was the bride watching when Ted kissed me? I look so nervous! **Above right:** Getting as close as I could to Steve Vizard after he had launched the programme of Leo Schofield's first Melbourne Festival (1994). **Below left:** Alan Finney and I swapping gossip (and possibly a kiss). **Below right:** Obviously hoping to seduce the head of Random House Australia, Ernest Mason, but I don't think he was fooled by our rubbing noses.

**Above left:** No, not an *argument* with the (then) French Ambassador Philippe Baude; just convincing him that, apart from Australia, the country I love most is France. **Top right:** Feeding Robert Carrier during his first visit to Australia in 1965 at Prunier's, Double Bay, and witnessed by the owner Tony Geminus. **Below left:** Sorry no details ... this is a secret. Photo taken at the Butterfly Ball in London during the 70s. I still have the mask but not the gentleman! **Below right:** I cannot recall what I was saying that so amused Frank Packer; but I do remember loving him, and shall never forget him.

**Above left:** A fun dinner party in eastern France, 1959, with important clients of Joseph Bancroft. Left to right: Hans Thomann of Taco, the late John Wendt of David Jones UK, Helen Rouff (my assistant in Paris) and Gilbert Rubod of Ets. Wallach. (I am next to Rubod but cannot imagine why I was ignoring the photographer.) **Above right:** 1959 in Paris with close Polish friend Michael Lis. **Below left:** In Tokyo 1968 with *Vogue* fashion editor Patricia dos Remedios, Trade Commissioner Desmond McSweeney and Mr T Kosuge, President of Isetan at the Australian Embassy reception for *Vogue* Australia. **Below right:** My pale blue Mini outside the garage at 39 Wolseley Road, Point Piper, 1962. I have no car in Victoria but have always kept my driver's licence current. I note that it is valid until 20 December 2001, in which case it may well outlive me!

**Above left and right:** Some naughty Frenchmen trying to turn me into a smoker while dining in 1959 with my chums Frank and Patsy Fox, who were staying with me in Paris. Left to right: Gilbert Rubod, myself, Frank Fox, Hans Thomann and Patsy Fox. (I did not like the taste of cigarettes and have never smoked.) **Below left:** I was the first *Vogue* editor to be a guest of honour at Hong Kong's Fashion Festival (1967) and was snapped for the press with this cute girl who had given me some flowers. **Below right:** With actor Donald Sinden (now Sir Donald) at the Victorian Arts Centre.

Above left: In London with American actor Elaine Stritch when I was contributing a monthly page to *Tatler* magazine during the 70s. Above right: With Sonia McMahon on Her Ladyship's 60th surprise birthday party at the Regent Hotel in Sydney. (Photo Robert Rosen) Below left: In 1985 with Dame Kiri Te Kanawa after the Victoria State Opera Foundation's gala benefit concert on 18 September in the Melbourne Concert Hall. Below right: With top Australian soprano Joan Carden when she won the Dame Joan Hammond Award. (Photo Robert Rosen)

**Above left:** I took this snap of one of my special liaisons, Jean Marc Baudoin, with whom I often went riding in the Forest of Fontainebleau. **Above right:** In the Carita Salon on the Faubourg St Honoré in Paris, having had my hair styled by one of the famous two sister-owners, the blonde Mlle Carita. (Photo courtesy *Vogue* Australia) **Below left:** At White City in Sydney with former Wimbledon champion Adrian Quist, a good friend and close neighbour of mine during the 60s in Point Piper. **Below right:** In the boutique of Paris couturier Hubert de Givenchy on avenue George V, with Givenchy himself (one of my favourite designers and amongst the most charming of men).

**Above left:** With Lord and Lady Harewood at the London launch of my *Bedside Cookbook* at New South Wales House in the Strand, 12 September 1979. **Above right:** HRH Prince Charles at a gala fundraising preview of *The Deep* at the Odeon cinema, Leicester Square, which I organised to raise money for the ENO Benevolent Fund. **Below left:** Early days on the Board of the VSO after a meeting at my home in South Yarra with the President the Earl of Harewood, the Chairman Jeffrey Sher QC, and Musical Director Richard Divall. **Below right:** Celebrating with Campbell McComas and Kate Boling at a party hosted by Dulcie Boling when the magazine *New Idea* (then under her editorship) had reached a circulation of 1 million copies per week.

**Opposite top:** The short, intimidating and powerful Helena Rubinstein between me and Ailsa Garland, then editor of British *Vogue*, in Paris, 1962. **Opposite centre:** Guest speaker at a VSO Foundation luncheon Anna Russell. **Opposite bottom:** With Dame Joan Hammond another guest speaker who helped raise money for the VSO.

**Above left:** 1958, Mascot Airport, as I was leaving Australia to live in Paris—holding my godson Anthony Potts. His mother Judy Barraclough was holding 'Matilda', a koala I later gave to André Courrèges. **Above right:** Anthony Potts aged seven (left) and Timothy Potts, aged three (now Director of the National Gallery of Victoria) with their mother at Jo Fallon's house in Vaucluse. **Below left:** With actor Lilli Palmer in London, 1976, at the launch of her autobiography *Change Lobsters and Dance*. **Below right:** Robert Carrier again—just because I love him. (Photo Bob Hart)

The late John Truscott AO, to whom I dedicate this book. Not a day passes without my thinking of this very special man. Alas, I knew him for only thirteen years. We met in Melbourne in 1980 and he died at the age of 57 in 1993.

This photo was taken at 'Raheen' during a fundraising luncheon and presentation of the Dame Mabel Brooks Award to Roxanne Hislop in October 1988. It was featured in Annette Allison's column in the *Sunday Telegraph* and is now one of the most treasured framed photographs in my apartment.

recognise fashion talent in this country.

In any field of endeavour in which creativity is the foundation, all great success stories started small. Therefore, why not use smaller designer firms as a testing ground for what you may consider as pilot runs one season, and eliminate some of the guess work that decides what will be the big runs for the volume market next year?

My advice is: seek out talent, foster it, back it, and finally profit from it. Let us use the Diors, Cardins and Courrèges of our own market—in other words, the trend setters—to spearhead the taste for the following season.

This principle of marketing applied equally, of course, to many other fields in which fabric yarns are used—such as furnishings, towellings, blankets, stockings, knitwear, etc. New ideas filter from the top; they always have done and always will do. Despite what one often heard—that we in Australia have no top, that we have neither the socio-economic structure nor the population to make this theory feasible—women are not equal when it comes to taste, fashion, their interests, nor are they uniform in their whole way of life. I went on:

Here in this country we now have a generation of young people who have grown up in an era of affluence, who have been well educated and many of whom have travelled or will have travelled before they settle down to their responsibilities. These are the people to whom we should appeal when thinking in terms of spearheading new trends and ideas.

I then made several key points about the quality of production in the Australian textile industry (good) and the quality of promotion (poor). I took, as an example, the menswear industry, which was doing particularly well at the time.

Why is it doing well? Because, as well as co-operating closely with the retailers the members themselves promote their look nationally (also internationally) and in this way create consumer demand through the stores. In turn the stores' own advertising of menswear (alone and co-operatively) is complementary but at no time the sole form of promotion. Now, if you as an industry really want to get up-to-date fashion to the public you must promote it. If your ideas are right the public will respond. This is not my opinion ... it is fact. As everyone knows, it is a highly successful formula in the fashion market of the United States.

I wanted to say a word about women in the textile industry—their place then, compared with what it could be. Believe me, I was not 'waving the flag' for my own sex. It has always been frankly immaterial to me whether a job is done by a man or a woman. But by the nature of the industry, and bearing in mind that most of its end products are ultimately bought by women, it was surely self-evident that qualified women could (and should be permitted to) play an important part in the creation and promotion of textile ranges.

If you agree with me that fashion is the catalyst that makes the industry move, then you should share my concern that there are not more women who understand fashion occupying positions of importance in the industry. Here again there are significant exceptions and a number of very able women have indeed made their mark. You will say that [suitably qualified people] are hard to find. Of course they are. Good people are always hard to find. But based on my own experience, there is not the slightest doubt in my mind that we have women with talent and potential who can be trained and who could become dedicated and productive forces in this industry, thus complementing the executive skills (so strongly masculine?) already developed by you over the years.

Every time I am in the United States, I am impressed by how many skilled women play an executive part in the creation and promotion of ranges, both as fashion directors and fashion co-ordinators. Here in Australia my colleagues and I at Vogue are constantly asked for advice and guidance, notably by firms who produce fabrics for women's fashion and yet do not have a woman in an important position on their staff. We love helping, and it is our duty to do so. But the problems presented to us are sometimes so basic, from a fashion point of view, that I cannot help thinking how much these particular firms would benefit if they had a capable fashion woman on their staff. In your own interests, therefore, I urge you to allow the different talents, drives, and enthusiasm that certain women possess to play an *important* part in the further development of your great industry.

I am a firm believer that all criticism should be constructive and that we should look for means to improve the way things are done. So I concluded my address to the textile industry representatives with some suggestions about where the future might lead us. I would like to re-offer these ideas today:

Shall we start an Australian Fashion Colour Council? By this I do not mean rival set-ups in Sydney or Melbourne, but a truly national body that is fully representative of the fashion industry. Should we also start a true Fashion Institute? This is an idea that I have thought about for some time ... one that I am especially aware of every time I am in the United States and notice the unanimity that exists in most seasons concerning the basics of fashion, namely colour and shape. This is largely brought about by a powerful and authoritative Fashion Group. This unanimity has tremendous influence on the public. It eliminates confusion in the consumer's mind and it makes last season's styles appear obsolete and makes women want to buy something new.

Here in Australia we have independent, often conflicting, promotions that frankly leave the public bewildered, and therefore inclined to say, 'Oh well, I'll make do with what I've got.' This is not exactly good for business. How much better if we had a national planning group to define a clear fashion picture twice a year. To have authority, it needs not only the *best* creative people connected with the textile and garment industries, but also the beauty people, the shoe people and of course the retailers. I am sure this can be done. So to take the idea further, should we not be thinking of showing twice a year, *to the public*, a composite collection of the right look in Australian fashion—the choice of garments to be shown chosen by this unbiased committee of experts? If this national planning group were truly 'non political' in the sense that it comprised only the best qualified from anywhere in Australia, its credibility and authority would be established quickly and the retail stores would be delighted to co-operate. So would the magazine and TV people, and without question the public would respond.

I only hope that some of my suggestions will spark off further ideas. Speaking on behalf of *Vogue* Australia, may I say that we have such confidence in the future of Australia that, in any way in which we can help this important industry, we shall be extremely proud to play our part.

> I confess that I appreciated the generous applause I received at the end of this speech, but what really pleased me was the fact that, from then on, many people from the textile industry found their way either to Bernard Leser's office or to mine.

My job was to 'sell' the acceptance of our strong fashion leadership in this country (not difficult in those days) and Leser's task was to persuade advertisers to back it (definitely not easy in those days, but he did it brilliantly). Many textile/fashion promotions were planned with Myer and David Jones and other retailers, which were beneficial to the whole industry as well as to Vogue Australia. Success was due to the fact that we maintained a highly respected Vogue office in Melbourne. Pat Carney headed the advertising department and Diana Crowther was our Melbourne editor.

Both Bernard Leser and I visited regularly and were known to all the retailers, designers, fabric houses and, most important of all, the advertisers and local press. Circulation increased. It was, remember, 47,500 when I left the magazine (the population was then only 8 million), so we had a good share of the market. In 1997 *Vogue*'s circulation was quoted in press articles as 72,000—which, in my opinion, with the population at 18 million, should have been higher ... but, as I have said, in my day as editor-in-chief there was really no competition from other glossy magazines (half my luck!) whereas, in the late 1990s, there is an abundance.

# 4

Elegance is good taste with a dash of daring.

**Carmel Snow**

# A Matter of Style

Early in 1967 Bernard Leser and I decided that we wanted (and Vogue needed) to obtain a bigger share of the advertising cake at the top end of the market. Our aim was to start a home-orientated magazine.

We were to have a problem over its title. Condé Nast Inc. already published *House & Garden* in the United States and in Britain, plus *Maison et Jardin* in France. Although they had protected their rights for the names in Europe, alas, they had neglected to do so in Australia. As a result someone had 'pinched' the title and had been publishing *Australian House and Garden* for a few years. Today, in my opinion, it is quite a good magazine; but then it was pretty mediocre. Printed on poor quality paper, with production to match, it contained editorials on 'how to put your carport up during the long weekend' and such. We were certainly not worried about it as competition but we did worry about its having what we considered to be a well-respected Condé Nast name! As it had been used for years without objection, we thought that a court case would not only be costly and lengthy, but possibly unwinnable, even by our brilliant Philadelphia lawyers. So it was planned that I would discuss our ideas with Iva Patcevitch and Alexander Lieberman during my coming visit to New York.

Pat (as he was known to us all) informed me that Condé

Nast still owned the title 'Living'. 'Why not start a *Vogue Living* magazine?' He went on to suggest 'On the cover start with "Vogue" in biggish letters above "Living". Later, when the circulation builds, drop the size of "Vogue" and make the word "Living" bold and big. Anyway think about it, but whatever you do, keep the word "Vogue" on the cover.'

We thought about it and settled for 'Vogue's Guide to Living'. The masthead had the words 'Vogue's Guide to' across the top of a big 'L I V I N G' stretched across the cover.

The first issue, Summer 1967, told our readers that this new quarterly magazine was going to be full of ideas for the house, for the garden and terrace, for men, for women and for children. To give you an accurate quote from our opening editorial page we said: 'It brings you, from our editors here and all over the world, the new trends in home architecture, decoration and landscaping. The best we see on the Australian market in furnishings and appliances ... chosen for quality and good taste. Good design at reasonable prices. Trend-setting ideas, practical ideas. Original ideas for entertaining, for enjoying leisure at home. A wealth of information from the experts. People ... where they go, what they do. Australian foods and wine. A big cook book.'

Apart from appointing a merchandise editor, there was no extra editorial budget for *Vogue Living* (eventually its shortened title). So all of us on *Vogue* Australia just worked harder and longer to put out the first few issues. Fortunately, being one of the Condé Nast family, we were able to 'lift' certain articles as well as stunning photographs from American and British *House & Garden*. This not only helped the staff situation, but strengthened our position in editorial leadership. It was our job to assist and encourage the general homewares industry to lift their standards, and to promote our own clever creative designers. There were plenty out there.

Looking back I must admit that giving birth to *Vogue Living* was a most exciting and satisfying time in my life. Never had I imagined that I would be the founding editor of a new publication. But I had a great team with me and the magazine took off. The advertisers loved it. We also had strong support from interior designers, architects, suppliers of furniture, fabrics, appliances, the food and wine industry and, most importantly, the retailers. Bernard and I were very happy because although we knew *we* needed the magazine, we now had proof that it was needed in the marketplace.

Later on we published bi-monthly and appointed Patsy Hollis as editor plus extra editorial staff. Formerly on my staff at *Vogue* Australia, Patsy was a top all-round writer, knew the importance of merchandising, was disciplined about our wretched deadlines, and got on well with people, including the production and art departments. She did a super job.

In 1969 I was invited to address the Sixth National Convention of the Housing Industry Association, which was to be held in Perth. This was, of course, a splendid opportunity to promote *Vogue Living*, both to the important trade delegates from all over Australia and to the public, hopefully future readers, in Western Australia. Patsy Hollis and a member of her staff Gail Heathwood persuaded me to accept, mainly by kindly offering to do a lot of research needed, and to help with the speech itself. They even suggested the title: 'Is the housing industry ignoring the basic needs of the Australian woman today?'

Many of the ideas I expressed in this address have since been taken up; but many have not, despite the passage of thirty years. For both of these reasons, I would like to share the substance of my speech with you now. Readers who are not particularly interested in opinions of magazine editors, nor magazines themselves, are urged to skip the rest of this chapter. Others, especially those with influence in the interior design field, might care to think about some of the issues raised.

I began by saying that I did not think it was the *'basic* needs' of Australian Women that the housing industry was ignoring. After all:

Walls, a roof and a floor are all that is absolutely necessary if we are referring to any literal definition of 'basic' in this context. Far more to the point, it is what that basic shell contains—the *details*—that are so patently neglected. And I believe the details are neglected partly because there are hardly any women employed in a decision-making capacity within the Australian Housing Industry.

There it was again—my precocious feminism. But, once more, I was merely dealing with facts. Of 218 graduates in the faculties of architecture in Australian universities in 1969, approximately sixteen per cent were women. Of the current design students, six per cent were women. I tossed these statistics at my audience, then asked:

How many of you in this audience employ women—even one woman—in key positions in your organisation? Or in fact at any level which might have a bearing on what goes into the *average* Australian home built for the *average* Australian woman?

Having given these chaps what I saw as the *cause* of the problem, I went on to spell out its exact *nature*.

The first problem area I want to examine is the distribution of space within the 50–60,000 new family dwellings built in Australia each year. The facts about the family social structure today are these. People are marrying younger and consequently starting families at an age at which their interests and activities are still those of *young* people. More wives and mothers are working or following other pursuits outside the home, in both young and middle-aged brackets, yet domestic help is the exception rather than the rule. All women, those who work and those who don't, are increasingly responsible to husbands and to children to be a social asset. In general terms, the pace of life is faster and a woman must give more of herself to keep up with its demands. Obviously, if she is to do this successfully, her first requisite is a well-planned home.

A well-planned house or home unit first of all means well-planned space: not just a division of so many squares into so many rooms; in other words, the *livability* of a dwelling is of prime importance.

I asked them to consider the kitchen as an example. A recently conducted *Vogue Living* survey had shown that ninety-two percent of readers were actively *interested* in cooking, meaning that they regarded cooking as a hobby as well as a duty.

But today cooking must be shared with a dozen other daily tasks. In my opinion this means that women want their kitchens to have the atmosphere of informal living rooms. In addition to adequate working and storage areas, women want space to serve sit-down meals. They want to be able to invite friends in for cups of coffee while something is cooking on the stove. They would like a desk in the kitchen where they can plan meals, make out grocery lists, talk to chums over the telephone, and make the business of running a home easier and more streamlined. In certain circumstances, such as multi-level houses, we know women who consider an intercom telephone in their kitchen a *necessity*.

I went on to talk about the laundry:

I realise that, according to all state and most local council building regulations, a laundry is a compulsory requirement in all new houses. Here again in my opinion laundries are not well-planned. Most are put in almost as an after-thought. You make a haphazard allowance for a tub, a washing machine and perhaps a dryer. Even if a woman uses her laundry once a day, that is all she does there and a laundry thus becomes an enforced area of largely wasted space. Please, if we must have separate laundries, let's make them good honest utility rooms with proper provision to store dirty linen, to fold clean clothes, to leave an ironing board permanently set up, to have mending requirements, perhaps even a sewing machine, handy. In fact, organised space for all the tasks a busy woman is expected to do to keep the family wardrobe and linen cupboard in working order.

Possibly the room that must make the biggest concession to our changing family life is the bedroom. The master bedroom, according to our recent surveys, is ideally a *retreat*—especially for couples with growing children—and as such should accommodate far more than the simple furniture of yesteryear. Today women want walk-in closets, a separate dressing area and bathroom (and I am going to say more about bathrooms in a minute or so), even room for a couple of easy chairs and a small coffee table. To give her these things need not add unreasonably to costs; it is simply a matter of planning for them.

Not only parents but children also (and teenagers especially) are demanding broader dimensions of bedrooms. The more 'doing your own thing' becomes important, the more the bedroom seems the place to do it. [...]

Now to get back to the bathroom. Here I shall be brief because what I have to say needs no explanation. I recently asked a cross-section of Australian women this question. 'Would you rather share a marble-lined elaborate bathroom with your family, or have a very simple bathroom all to yourself?' Invariably each woman's plea was for a separate bathroom, however basic—anything that would give her uninterrupted privacy to relax over bathing and grooming without having to wait in a queue to get it. This also applies, I am sure, to fathers. So why, in the 1970s is *any* bedroom built without its own bathroom?

What I want to say next might offend many delegates here today. I must, however, state that we—that is, my staff, *Vogue Living* readers and Australian women generally—believe the housing industry as a whole ignores the well-researched information that would enable it to improve the efficiency, comfort and safety of Australian homes. Architects, builders, those who supply materials and fittings, manufacturers of home appliances—you are equally guilty.

Efficiency, for example. It has been estimated that the average housewife walks 730 miles (now 1175km) a year in the course of her duties: that she spends 75.5 minutes every weekday at the sink and 26.9 minutes in front of the stove. It also seems that a large number of her common physical ailments, such as back aches, varicose veins and so on, are due to badly planned houses equipped with inefficiently designed appliances and fittings. Those who build and equip houses seem content to make a guess, an educated one perhaps but nevertheless a guess, at the standards on which they base their designs, instead of taking the time and money to conduct their own time-and-motion studies or their own research into such subjects as ergonomics and anthropometrics at a domestic level. As I have said, you even ignore the resources of those independent organisations who would willingly supply such information. Thousands of dollars are spent each year to improve the lot of workers in *industry*, yet to make equivalent improvements in the lot of the worker at home (and every woman in this country between the ages of 18 and 85 spends some part of her day on household chores) you members of the housing industry hardly lift a finger.

Here, I felt that I should offer some constructive pointers.

I know that one of the functions of the HIA is an *economic* research division. So why not an operation and methods research division as well? I know, too, that a number of you do employ your own researchers. Why not combine forces? Or once again, why not use the resources that are available to you? Over the last few months I have spoken to many of these research organisations, those established by the state and commonwealth governments, by universities, by market research companies and design groups. I was told they publish regular bulletins and papers on their findings, but these publications receive far greater attention from members of fellow organisations than from the HIA. I learned, too, that of the number of requests for information that come to these organisations, each year, nearly *half* as many come from the public as from those concerned with building and equipping domestic dwellings. Which is like the teacher doing half the pupil's homework. In fact, I could say the same thing of *Vogue Living*. We receive frequent requests from readers for information about fitments, building materials and appliances, *and* many complaints. Yet I cannot remember the last time an architect, builder or manufacturer asked us what readers thought about these things. I am told that, of the overall millions of dollars spent by the housing industry in Australia each year, less than one per cent goes into research. I cannot help but believe that this figure is correct.

Having made my viewpoint as clear as possible, I gave my patient listeners an opportunity for retribution. I had compiled a list, from readers' correspondence and from my own sources, of general complaints and of possible remedies. I urged these men, for the sake of their wives and daughters, to listen with an open mind while I took some minutes to go through this detailed list. It included: working heights (of sinks, benches and floor appliances)—raise them, custom build, or make them adjustable; waste disposal units—these were indispensable and should be mass-produced to make them inexpensive; acoustics—soundproofing should be a standard feature in all homes; airconditioning—install it in homes, just as we had done in cars; heights of windows and door handles—raise the former (for child safety and furniture placement) and lower the latter (for child safety); forward planning—design in a flexible way to allow for future changes; electrical circuits and service equipment—ensure that these are plentiful and well placed; security—provide for alarms at the *planning* stage, and instal locks on *all* external doors and windows; fire precautions—tile around stoves, place fire extinguishers conveniently, avoid use of flammable building materials, use only air vents with flaps so that they can be closed, provide plugs for downpipes to trap water in gutterings, and install sprinkler systems that can spray roofs.

The delegates (and some wives) at this National Convention of the Housing Industry Association had not gone to sleep, so I went on. In case they were inclined to raise costs as an objection, I pointed out the statistics, which showed that women were instrumental in choosing a particular house for its efficiency, comfort and safety as much as for its looks. Then I added up the savings for them, broadly speaking:

The more the members of the Housing Industry co-operate with one another in research and production areas to give her these things, the lower the cost of them will be. The lower the cost, the more of these improvements (improvements suggested by your market, remember) you will be able to incorporate in the houses you build and equip. And the better the houses you build at a reasonable cost to the purchaser, the more houses you will sell, and the greater the prosperity of the housing industry in Australia.

Next, I addressed what I called 'changing fashions in living'.

It seems to me that, after a long period of rashly adopting any new fashion or trend another country cared to toss our way—Britain, America, the Continent, we are establishing (or perhaps re-establishing if you consider our very distinguished post-colonial years) a lifestyle that is all our own. While we have learned a lot from other countries, and I am sure we will continue to learn, we now seem to have enough national confidence to reject influences that hinder our emerging national character. It shows not only in our cultural, commercial and political endeavours, but in the ways in which we choose to relax and entertain. In home entertaining, we are moving outdoors and this general change affects your industry— especially the architects, builders and developers amongst you. As part of our houses we want functional patios, courtyards and a revival of those wide-eaved verandas of colonial days. As part of our high-rise developments, we want balconies that are more than the pocket-handkerchief ornamental affairs that predominate today. We want roof gardens and community parks and playgrounds.

As my next point, I returned to the analogy between houses and cars. Cars come equipped with a string of optional extras; with each one that you reject on purchase, the lower the purchase price. To me this seemed the next logical step to take for project houses—that is, semi-mass-produced houses designed with such things as barbecue pits, courtyards, swimming pools, at a fixed starting price that *dropped* as you eliminated the extras. I knew that this idea had been most successful overseas, for both buyer and seller. It was one we could adopt here without undue difficulty if someone found the courage to start the ball rolling.

To finish, I looked ahead—with quite some foresight, I now realise.

In the next ten years, I believe that fashions in living will change even more dramatically than they have to date. Take marriage, for instance. With the widespread use of the contraceptive pill and the greater opportunities for women to make a full-time career out of their chosen profession, marriage could possibly become less and less the order of the day. Although this generation might not yet be willing to accept the idea, even today we have young men and women who prefer to live in mixed community groups rather than as couples. And today if a single woman can prove her earning capacity, she can obtain finance to buy her own house or apartment with comparatively little trouble. So, in the next ten years, I feel both these contingencies—communal living and the woman who chooses to remain single—will need to be catered for by the housing industry. Since neither of these needs will be the same as family housing needs, designers and manufacturers could be facing a whole new market area, and looking for a whole new set of ideas. I wonder if they will be ready ...

Something else that occurs to me about the future of housing: will houses be portable enough, even disposable enough, to suit the attitude

of coming generations? The last two or three years have seen the introduction to Australia of plastic furniture and pre-packaged portable
houses. You might remember an article in the first issue this year of
*Vogue Living* about the fibreglass Futuro house from Finland, which is
now available in Australia ... and these things would seem to indicate
that the coming generation is seeking a new freedom in its housing.

I left my distinguished audience with the question 'Has
the housing industry looked ahead to what the next step
might be in this direction?' and invited them to discuss (with
Patsy Hollis or myself) any visions they thought worthwhile.
We would publish them in a future edition of *Vogue Living*.

Anyone who has read the last two chapters may already
be comparing the situation today, now that there is such a
broad range of lifestyle and fashion magazines available. The
editors, what is more, have such an exciting market from
which to select for their fashion, beauty and homeware pages.

I feel envious ... but I also feel proud. There is no question that *Vogue*'s influence all those years ago made this happen. We did raise the standards. Our leadership set the taste,
we guided and advised both consumers and wholesale traders.
We boosted sales with stylish promotions, strongly backed by
merchandise with leading retailers—all under the 'As seen in
*Vogue*' umbrella. Our fashion editors *looked* the part as well
as being passionate about clothes and accessories.

My views have not changed much, nor has my lifestyle!
I still maintain that a *Vogue* reader looks for good taste in
both fashion and beauty guidance *basically*, plus leadership
for what is best value for money. She may like to be shocked
occasionally by way-out clever photographs. That's OK, as

long as they are not in bad taste. As Carmel Snow, the famous founding editor of *Harper's Bazaar*, said, 'Elegance is good taste with a dash of daring.'

On 27 May 1970 I received a formal letter from Government House, Sydney, advising me that Her Majesty the Queen would be conferring on me—for services to journalism and commerce—the award of Member of the Most Excellent Order of the British Empire (MBE) ... this information *not* to be divulged to anyone prior to the announcement of the Birthday Honours on the long weekend of 13 June 1970.

I was totally surprised but absolutely thrilled—except for the fact that I thought the honour, as I said earlier in this book, should have gone to the whole of Vogue's team. While I did not even tell my parents, I did confide in a special friend who ran the National Trust shop. She kindly arranged to open it secretly on the Monday (a public holiday) so that I could purchase small gifts and handwrite personal cards to all my colleagues. She also arranged to have them delivered by 9am, before I got to my office, on the Tuesday morning. Each card had a big M for Mainly, B for Because of, E for Everyone's efforts, and was signed 'Love S.S.'

Back in 1962, when the official agreement had been finalised with Condé Nast Inc. New York concerning my appointment as editor of *Vogue* Australia and *Vogue* New Zealand, I received a prompt cable from Bernard Leser 'To convey my delight and to send you my heartiest congratulations.' A follow-up air letter soon arrived at my Paris address, in which

Leser wrote, 'I simply want to tell you how immensely I am looking forward to your arrival and to working with you in "double harness" '—which I thought was a great way to describe the way management should work with editorial.

As it happened, this 'double harness' attitude worked very well for a number of years. Leser and I were both directors of Condé Nast Australia but he was the managing director, so senior to me. In time, he was to invoke his hierarchical superiority.

I have never hesitated to make it clear that I do not respect rank, only ability. I certainly had great admiration for Leser's ability on the advertising and sales side of the business, but did not, as I say, respect rank. This understandably was resented. I felt strongly that the lifeblood of any magazine was its editorial content and have not changed my views. Eventually, after nine years with Vogue and quite a few differences of opinion (a euphemism for rows with Bernie), I resigned in 1971. It was what you might call a 'forced resignation', but then that was par for the course in the world of magazines and newspapers. It still is today, come to think of it.

Bernard Leser was very ambitious and there is nothing wrong with that. He went on to make a distinguished career with Condé Nast in the US, the UK, Europe and the Pacific. But we did not part as friends, and for quite a while I would not shake his hand. In fact, in 1986 I was quoted in the *National Times* as saying 'He didn't have instinctive style. I think it is extraordinary that he doesn't credit what we did for him in creating a base for all he has achieved.' Not a nice thing to say; I was still resentful. But, as Neil Shoebridge wrote in the 1 May 1995 issue of the *Business Review Weekly*, quoting a rival magazine publisher, 'Like all good magazine executives, Bernie is an expert at self-promotion. As a result, he sometimes forgets to give credit where credit is due.'

I am happy to tell you that for a good many years now we have been good friends.

After I had left Condé Nast, nearly every day my mail contained letters galore (by galore I mean fifty to eighty all told, and I have kept them all these years). These letters came not only from Australia but from all over the world—from colleagues on other Condé Nast publications, radio and press people, fashion designers and buyers, retail directors, photographers and models, many many subscribers to both *Vogue* and *Vogue Living* magazines—and, believe it or not, even a few advertisers with whom, as editor, I had shared a love/hate relationship. I have to confess that the contents of these letters gave me great joy at the time and I felt like sending copies of them to Leser ... but didn't. On reflection I realise that there could perhaps have been the odd character who was happy to know I had left (I like to think not many!) but they never put it in writing ... at least not to me.

The letter I treasured most was from a woman for whom I had the highest respect: my associate editor on both magazines, Elizabeth Reeve. We editorial staff worked late-ish hours, often leaving the office well after 7 o'clock. Liz Reeve was always the last to leave and on 31 May 1971 at 8pm she wrote to me on Vogue letterhead:

I'm feeling so very sad. Rather weepy and dammit, nobody seems to have any Kleenex. After the grace note of this morning—your warm flower-bearing letter—for

Vogue to let you softly-and-silently-vanish-away (like the Boojum!) seems so ungracious, so boorish and ungrateful ... although I know you expressly forbade a big speeches-plus farewell scene. Hard to say in words that don't sound soppy, so I want to write what should be said: how much I've enjoyed and learned working with you ... what pleasure it has been to have an incorruptible editor always welling with ideas, always enthusiastic, always keeping up the standards that Condé Nast set for Vogue. Standards I fear may well be phased out by new management generations who put expediency ahead of 'style' in all things. There are so many kindnesses, so many generous gifts (I'm surrounded by them at home!) which I owe to you, which I thank you for. My return look at Ireland the latest but not least among them (a very unsettling one). It was my good luck and privilege, at the time when my own life had been newly shattered, to have you come along to order my working days.

You have put up over the years with my grumpiness, chronic pessimism, parochial outlook, and given me nine years of fun and excitement and travel I would never have expected at the time to have again. So, God bless—and may the most remarkable woman I know (that's not a glib phrase. I've thought about it and cannot come up with any serious competitor) have as much luck and happiness in the next nine years, and many more. And after that hi falutin' note, will you come to lunch at 49 Crown Street (entrance yellow door on Broughton St—*you* know) next Saturday? Or

Sunday? Or dinner on either day, if it suits you better.
Just us chickens. And may we ever stay good friends.
(Sorry for all this bad typing, but it's easier on you than
my terrible non-handwriting!) Much love Elizabeth (Liz).

I still treasure an anonymous poem that was popped in
among some papers as I was leaving the offices of Vogue for
good. I read it in my good friend Frank Packer's Bentley.
Frank had insisted on sending his chauffeur to 49 Clarence
Street. 'Scotter, you leave in style. Don't let the bastards get
you down—and come and have a good lunch.' I showed him
the poem:

Now I just can't believe it,
After the good things, the bad
And the long stretches,
I remember now, of course,
The sunny days in early summer
When she came in in white silk,
Summer sandals,
The harbour danced with sun,
The ships below were setting off
For tropical places,
And our magazine was gathering up
All that was juicy and alive
On the local scene.

Now it is over. That phase is over.
The room is suddenly tatty,
And dirty on the walls where
The pictures have come down

And the dresser taken away.
Miss Scotter puts the last
Red carnation in the tall bottle
With two other flowers ... making
For once, and never before,
A clumsy mixture, a left over.
She picks up her big black
Crocodile bag and says something
To fill the last space as it empties.

# 5

A successful marriage is not a gift; it is an achievement.

**Ann Landers**

No matter how happily a woman may be married, it always pleases her to discover that there is a nice man who wishes she were not.

**H L Mencken**

# Marriages and Other Liaisons

When I was writing my weekly column for 'Melbourne Living' in the *Age* newspaper, I was asked to judge a competition in a special bridal supplement to be published on 3 October 1983. The question for competitors was: 'Apart from love, what are five essential ingredients that make a successful marriage?' The winner was to be given a luxurious holiday in Hawaii for seven nights plus return air fares for two people. In advance, I had been asked to enumerate the five points that *I* considered to be essential. Entries that included any of my points were to go into a barrel from which I was to pick the winner.

I duly listed my essential ingredients:
- a lasting respect for each other
- sexual compatibility
- a similar sense of humour
- a tolerant attitude towards each other's family relations
- total loyalty.

They were, I thought, good ingredients, but—mind you—I was sixty-two years of age then and considerably wiser than when I first became engaged to be married, at the age of twenty-one, to a handsome young Royal Naval officer.

Geoffrey Batten-Pearce and I were married on 19 December 1942 (I'd just turned twenty-two). It was during

World War II. I was hopelessly in love with this man of the same age, but I had no judgement, my values were all wrong and I was a typically confused English virgin. (In those days well-brought-up girls did not 'sleep around' before marriage. Personally I would suggest young people always try out sex well before getting married, not that the young of today need such advice!) In terms of my five ingredients, the marriage was a disaster. I started losing respect for my husband—partly because of our sexual *in*compatibility but also because I found out that he was a gambler. While I liked, and have to this day remained close friends with, his youngest sister Carol Stratton, I soon became intolerant of the rest of his family and my bossy mother-in-law was not particularly tolerant of me— but then I had married her favourite son. After about two years I decided to leave. So no marks for loyalty, Scotter—and our senses of humour were not entirely similar. When I told my parents that I had left Geoffrey there was not exactly the sympathy I expected. Instead of 'Oh you poor darling, what happened?' my Mama said, 'Sheila, we have never had a divorce in the family.'

When Geoffrey went to live in New York and wanted to marry again, he managed to get our marriage annulled in the British High Court of Justice without my having to make an appearance. The case was heard in camera on 4 January 1950.

By the time the news reached me (about six years after I had left my husband), I had also left England and was living in Melbourne. During those intervening years I had enjoyed more than a few romantic 'liaisons' and was making an interesting career in fashion, loving my freedom and certainly not planning to marry again.

In 1951 I was being courted by Alan Ford McIntyre, head of Pan American Airways in Victoria. Although I was falling in love with him, when he asked me to marry him I suggested that, with my track record, we should live together. (My dear old parents would have had a fit! To them such arrangements amounted to 'living in sin'—the word *relationship* had a totally different meaning in those days and only solicitors, stockbrokers, bridge players and so on were called 'partners'.) Being a happy independent woman way ahead of my time, I was scared of a second marriage. I knew I was not good wife material; I really should have stayed single all my life. Alan thought differently. He had not been married, his widowed mother (whom he adored) was living in Melbourne, and he insisted we marry. So, on 11 September 1951, we were married quietly and privately in the Office of the Government Statist, Queen Street, Melbourne. I was thirty-one years old.

The next day the Melbourne *Herald* newspaper wrote 'Marriage was best-kept secret of week' as a headline, followed by 'Style expert Sheila Scotter has certainly turned out to be the darkest horse of the season. She slipped out of her High Fashion Salon in Myer on Tuesday afternoon without a word to a soul and proceeded to become Mrs Alan McIntyre with the minimum of fuss and ado. A few of her close friends were in the know and two of these, Betty and Leo Frankel, gave a party for the newly-weds later in the afternoon, at which the bombshell burst. Sheila is the only daughter of Mr and Mrs H G Scotter of Oaktree Cottage, Ringwood, Hampshire, England, and Alan the younger son of the late Mr W G McIntyre and of Mrs McIntyre of Berkeley Street Hawthorne [sic].'

Perhaps it was not a good omen that I wore a black linen suit … but it *was* Balenciaga! However, we scored pretty well concerning those five (no mention of love, remember) ingredients for success. We definitely had respect for each other and we shared a sense of humour. We were also mutually loyal. As for family relations, Alan did not have to worry about mine: he never met them. I liked his Mama very much and we got on, though I know that secretly she did not approve of 'working wives' and certainly not one who put her career before giving birth to children.

Fortunately for me, this second husband had no interest in children. I am positive that I would not have been a very good parent in this country, where I observed so many women working hard, and devoting most of their free time to what I call 'waiting on' their children. I admired them for this but was more in favour of a British nanny training and boarding school.

I remember, when I was in my forties and living in Sydney, thinking seriously about adopting a Vietnamese boy orphan. Tony Larkins QC, a wise old chum, talked me out of it. 'You are not really thinking about the child,' he said. 'Imagine how that kid is going to be teased at school, being labelled Miss Scotter's son, with no father. You are just being selfish, my dear, and not very practical.' He was quite right.

Alan and I had a good and satisfying sex life, but it was never my priority, so that when I was offered an important new job which meant moving first to Sydney then to Paris to live, I accepted without consulting my husband. Inevitably this did not go down too well. A divorce was eventually granted to Alan on the grounds of desertion and refusal of conjugal rights, the notice having been 'served' on me in Paris, dated 29 October 1959. (The decree nisi was granted in June 1960.)

We remained firm friends. He did not re-marry and when I flew back to live in Melbourne (arriving on Boxing Day, 1979) he met me at Tullamarine and drove me to the converted stable I had bought in Millswyn Place, South Yarra. I had planned just to camp in the place while all my goods and chattels were coming by sea, so brought only my favourite sharp knife and wooden spoon. Alan thoughtfully lent me a bed and, amazingly, produced some of my china from our married days, plus some useful kitchen items which he had stored 'In case you ever came back'. We saw each other quite a lot but seldom with other friends of mine; although an interesting and attractive man, he really was an anti-social bloke. A very heavy smoker, he died from emphysema. At his request I did not visit him in hospital.

If there were a school-type report on marriage, I would not get high marks. I confess that I made little effort to make either of mine work, and I pray that the Good Lord will forgive me for breaking sacred vows. In my youth I had never heard the word *feminist* but I think I must have been one since the age of five, and even during childhood was always more of a leader than a follower. Later in life I was pretty self-determined and valued independence. Now, in this much-later-in-life period, I still feel the same.

Way back in June 1969 I was interviewed by Elizabeth Riddell for a series of articles she was writing in the *Australian* newspaper entitled 'Women On Their Own'. When she arrived at my apartment in Point Piper, Sydney, I had just hung up from a call from an American beau of mine. When I told him I was about to be questioned as to why I lived on my own, he said, 'There's no secret about that. Nobody could possibly live with you.'

Riddell knew that I had been married twice, and asked whether I thought of trying again. I told her:

The only sort of man I could marry would be one who was absolutely successful and who needed a woman like me—an ambassador perhaps—but then I would rather be the ambassador myself. I do not mind coming home to an empty flat. I need a good deal of time on my own, more than I get now. [I was busy being editor-in-chief of *Vogue* Australia and *Vogue Living* at the time.] I like to have the flat to myself. I don't want a man in the kitchen or the bathroom. There are many women who at my age [forty-eight then] get re-married or stay married to have an escort. It's unimportant to me. I warn friends not to invite a boring male just to make up the numbers at dinner, and I am quite happy to turn up at parties on my own.

That day I also informed Elizabeth Riddell that women like me want a special private life, on our own terms and according to our own timing. If one is discreet this does not preclude the odd romance or 'liaison'. (I prefer this word to 'affair'. 'Liaison' has several meanings. In France, to me it meant intimacy, yet to cooks *'faire une liaison'* meant to thicken a sauce.) I would not have a romance in which I had to be continually conniving, and in a small place like Sydney a woman on her own was so vulnerable to gossip.

Luckily I travel overseas quite frequently, so am able to catch up with people I'm fond of in Europe and the United

States. I have managed to stay friends with my old loves, even maintaining regular exchanges of letters. Yet this does not mean I agree with cynical old George Bernard Shaw who said 'The ideal love affair is one conducted by post.' (Gosh, dear GBS, how darn dull the whole thing would be, carried on through the mail!) However, when it comes to prolonging a romance from a long distance, believe me, letters from former liaisons are a great joy—both exciting and mentally stimulating. But if one wants to be the recipient of such billets-doux, then one must be prepared to bloomin' well write fairly regularly oneself. This I always found easy to do.

While living in Australia I have kept in touch, exchanging public news, and sharing private memories with favourite men I have loved in France, England and the United States ... oh, and one in New Zealand. These days, thoughts and messages can be exchanged through secret fax and private telephone numbers—not quite as romantic as a handwritten love letter, but instant contact with the other side of the world, although I am always terrified that I may have dialled the wrong fax number.

---

While I can hardly call myself a virtuous woman, I have never indulged in casual sexual relationships. I do admit, however, that, had I been hot-blooded and highly sexed, I most probably would have been promiscuous in my youth, middle age ... even later perhaps! While flirtations were frequent and fun over the years, the fact is I only ever achieved true sexual happiness with a man when I was genuinely in love. Curiously, on looking back, I usually only fell in love with a bloke who was in love with me—or well on the way to being so. Was this practicality, or vanity—or perhaps a little of both?

In my strict British upbringing, my parents told me that good manners were a combination of education, intelligence, taste and style. Bearing this in mind, it would be appalling manners to name the two men with whom I have had serious and long-lasting liaisons, true, deep and meaningful. The initial meeting with each of these beloved gentlemen was in Australia, to be followed later by many many more in England and France over a number of years. Each was quite happily married with children. I knew it was morally wrong to allow the loves to grow, but I did not start the romance in either case, merely giving in to courtship and seduction without protest, and can look back without regret on the happiest years of my life.

Rules were made so that no one got hurt and we just savoured times we could spend together. This suited me as I had no intention of changing my single status or losing my freedom. I never waited in for telephone calls, for example, and seldom worried about what went on when either of these men left me.

I have often pondered what my life would have been like had I met either of these men when I was in my twenties ... one typically English, the other typically French. Would I have married one of them? ... A hypothetical question. The answer? Yes, and I would have spent the rest of my life in France.

To leave Paris in 1962 to take up the exciting challenge of editing *Vogue* Australia in Sydney was an easy decision from a career point of view but my heart certainly did not approve. I still have the letter written to me at the time of my departure, which ended 'Fortunately you left on Friday. Two days of your presence can be considered a vaccine against a disease. A third day and I would have caught it, and would have been violently ill again. Yes, you are a beloved poison inoculated through my ears, my eyes, my thoughts so deeply that the quality of your presence does not vanish when you have left. Darling Sheila, God bless you and the decisions you may have to take in the near future.'

---

Back in 1956 on the very day on which Prince Phillip was to open the Melbourne Olympic Games, I boarded a Pan American flight in Sydney—my destination, Honolulu. Understandably hardly anyone was leaving the country on what was such an auspicious day for Australia. In fact, I was only one of three passengers in first class and from memory I think the crew were two to one. Were we pampered? You bet.

I was flying to Hawaii to be with the beau in my life at the time, one Bernard Goodman. I had met him only a few months earlier in New York on a business trip, just after I had started a new job working for Joseph Bancroft of Wilmington, Delaware, USA. (As you have read, I was director of their marketing division for Australia and New Zealand, for their trademarks 'Banlon' and 'Everglaze Minicare.') One of their UK directors, Nathan Clarke, who was pretty 'clued up' on the fashion-cum-textile scene in the States, introduced us, having informed me that Goodman's company, Sportwhirl Inc., was one of the most important manufacturers of sportswear and leisure wear on the market.

I confess that I liked Bernard Goodman immediately. Apart from being tall, stylish and distinguished looking, he had the most wonderful sense of humour, which I attributed to his Russian–Jewish background. We dated (to use the American term) several times that week and during my return from London on my way back to Sydney. It was obvious that we were both happy in each other's company, in spite of my 'no sex please, I'm British' attitude—well, that was his (teasing) interpretation! I thought to myself, 'being an eligible, fairly rich bachelor in the Big Apple this guy must have plenty of women in his life so don't let yourself get involved ... well, not *too* involved!'

At the airport, seeing me off, Bernard proposed that we should plan to see each other soon. 'Why not come back to New York on holiday?' he asked. 'Why don't you come over to Sydney?' said I. But like most New Yorkers of his era, Bernard did not relish long distance flights, and New York was the only place in the world to live.

Eventually, after many telephone calls to Sydney (he hated writing letters), he compromised. If I would fly to Honolulu to meet him, he would plan a holiday to coincide with mine and we could get to know each other during three weeks. We did. And it was one of the most fabulous holidays I have ever had. Honolulu in 1956 was very different from how it is today. There were very few tourists (even Waikiki Beach was uncrowded) and only three or four major hotels. There was hardly any traffic and in my opinion it was a rather romantic place. It was certainly a very romantic place *in which to be courted* (I was) and to fall in love (I did).

During those three weeks Bernard and I discussed marriage. I say 'discussed' because Bernard's proposal was conditional that I move to New York—not only because of his business commitments (which I could understand completely) but because he said that he would *never* live anywhere else and certainly not in Australia, where I wanted to live the rest of *my* life. The nearest Bernard got to Australia was when we went over to the big island, Hawaii, also known as the orchid island, one weekend. We stayed together at the picturesque old fashioned Kona Inn, almost on the water's edge at Kailua Bay. I was given a heavy gold bracelet in lieu of an engagement ring (having been married twice, engagement rings were hardly my scene). I have worn this bracelet almost every day since. It was always too long and eventually (almost thirty years later) I took it to Maker's Mark in Melbourne and had one of their designers take out two links and make them into matching earrings. (Many of my chums may be bored with both bracelet and earrings by now, as I am still wearing them—and still enjoy them.)

Much as I loved this man, I knew deep down in my heart that I would never be a suitable wife for him. After all, I had not made much effort to overcome problems in my two former marriages and I frankly had to admit to myself that I enjoyed being single. In his heart I think Bernard did too. At the time when we met, I was thirty-six years old and he was forty-two. We remained the closest of loving friends for over thirty-five years, during which time, whenever I visited New York, nearly all my free time was spent with him and with his brother Arthur and his adorable sister-in-law Betty

Goodman. Although all three were colleagues in Sportwhirl Inc., they were extremely close buddies and enjoyed each other's company.

When not on what I call 'an expenses-paid business trip', I always stayed in Bernard's New York apartment at 9 East 67th Street. During summer we would weekend at the Goodman beach house complex (two modern family-friendly timber houses separated by a communal swimming pool) right on the edge of the beach at Quogue on Long Island.

I soon realised why Goodman got on so well with Aussies. His sense of humour matched theirs in most cases. I remember one Saturday when he told me that he had seen the movie *Crocodile Dundee* nine—yes, nine—times! And he insisted on dragging me to see *Crocodile Dundee II* one sunny afternoon, on Long Island of all places. Fond as he was of my compatriots, I was still unsuccessful in persuading him to visit Sydney. However, when I was resident in Paris (1958–1962) and later in London (1971–1980) he did cross the Atlantic from time to time and got to know quite a few French and English friends of mine as well as the many Australians who kept in touch with me on their travels. Likewise he introduced me to many interesting and talented Americans in the fashion, textile and finance circles, many of whom remain my friends today.

I was always grateful for Bernard's advice concerning my own career in fashion. I can recall, way back in 1960/61, Goodman's vision of what could be a commercially successful deal between leading retailers and the Paris couture houses. (Remember I am talking of almost forty years ago.) He told me that he could never understand the reticence of the French designers. 'Why don't they invade the vast American market with commercially sound arrangements for reproduction under franchise or licence? Instead they let stores and manufacturers buy an original garment (admittedly at an expensive price) with the right to copy it entirely, or part of it such as the new collar, the way the sleeve is put in, the special new cut of a jacket or skirt, and so on.'

He was right. According to the rules of the French *Chambre Syndicale de la Couture* (their trade union, in other words), garment manufacturers from foreign countries paid a few thousand dollars and made a written commitment to purchase X number of garments before they were let in to view a winter or summer Paris collection. This was probably peanuts to some of the important wholesale Seventh Avenue manufacturers, yet they could make millions of dollars from the sale of copies to retail stores all over the United States.

We discussed this quite frequently, and Bernard knew about my friendship with the multi-talented designer André Courrèges. Although Courrèges was the hot ticket for new fashion ideas at the time, his financial standing was certainly not in the 'what-shall-we-do-with-all-this-money?' class. Bernard suggested that I approach him and show him how he could make a fortune in the US and eventually the world. I knew that André was one of those many artists whose philosophy is not dollar driven and I explained this to Bernard. He urged me to approach him all the same, outlining his proposal in the following letter:

## Sunday

Spending a delightful weekend at the beach. The weather is simply delightful and I'm more convinced than ever that I will never leave the U.S. in the summer again if can help it. I hope that you are enjoying yourself and that all goes well. From the newspapers I get the impression that the Collections have been quite dull. I do hope that you do get the opportunity to discuss business with your friend. I believe that my concept will make so much more money than has ever been made before by a French designer, Dior notwithstanding.

Roughly darling, my thought is to bring into the fold roughly 50 stores to begin with. Don't mention it but I've already spoken to Jay Rossbach [head of Saks at the time] and I am sure it can be done. My idea is to set up complete departments selling only his [Courrèges'] designs ... coats, suits, dresses, knits, boots, sportswear etc. The clothes to be manufactured here in the U.S. by outstanding manufacturers that I will select and who already have tremendous distribution and a good product. Therefore there will be absolutely no cost to him, other than the original sketches and designs. He can continue to sell to his private customers if he wishes but this is so small at this point as far as the U.S. is concerned.

Bernard then set down the financial details, using rough estimates. His conclusion:

the pie for us and Mr C would amount to $2,500,000 for which we have very little financial investment or danger. As you can readily see every $10,000,000 would mean another $500,000 as our share. I'm sure this sounds ridiculous but I feel that I am being conservative in my estimates because we would be dealing with outstanding stores and manufacturers. My feeling is that this is the only direction for him to go. I think that you could do the same for England, Australia and Canada etc.

Needless to say I am prepared to offer him minimum guarantees etc. but I do want it understood that I would take charge of everything this end. Think about this, speak with him and keep me informed. Time is of the essence and I believe that this new concept would set the retail fashion business on its proverbial ear.

I'll try to call you next week after you have received my letter. If anything is vital call me at the office or at home. She-She [my nickname] pursue this as best you can. I see tremendous possibilities for us all. I'm running out of paper and missing the sun! Adieu my She-She, be well and enjoy yourself. Keep me posted regarding your plans please. Love Bernardo.

P S Darling try not to give too much information, figures, stores already interested etc. unless you feel they can be trusted not to by-pass us.

I have to report that, in spite of my friendship with

André Courrèges, I could not persuade him—and I did try. Rightly or wrongly—and personally I think wrongly—he declined this deal, expressing his scepticism about the ways of doing business in America.

Incidentally romantic thoughts and memories of Bernard Goodman came back to me in 1997 while on holiday at the blissful Four Seasons Resort Hualalai, on Hawaii. I flew to join Ruth Woolard, whom I call my American/New York sister, and her family, who were vacationing in this (then) new luxury hotel and golfers' paradise. Ruth, who knew Bernard and knew of our romance, sensed that I would want to go and have a look at Kona. We drove there from Hualalai. Oh dear ... no longer any quaint old Kona Inn. I suppose after so many years, I should have expected this formerly charming and peaceful tropical little place to have changed. The only thing I recognised was a magnificent old banyan tree, which was still flourishing but surrounded by a bustling tourist complex, parking lots, souvenir shopping plazas, and condominiums galore. Lots of happy people were enjoying themselves, but I doubt that any of them could trump my reflections on such a happy past spent in this place.

It is said one should never look back but coincidentally part of my Hawaiian island holiday was also spent with someone whom I call my American/Honolulu sister, Alberta Gillette Liljestrand. It was Bernard Goodman who first introduced us over thirty years ago and we have been like sisters ever since. Alberta lives with her husband Howard in Honolulu, Oahu ... well, that is the postal address but to reach their magical house in Tantalus Drive one drives up a winding tree-clad road to about 600 metres above sea level.

It is what I like to call their 'tree house', with breathtaking views over Honolulu to Diamond Head on one side and Pearl Harbour on the other. There is not another house to be seen from their private tropical garden ... I think that Goodman would agree with me that the Liljestrand property is 'para-disiacal'—the description we gave to Honolulu in 1956. When I commented on the traffic and crowds in Waikiki these days, Alberta told me that Honolulu was now the twelfth largest city of the United States, and that's why they live on Mount Tantalus.

---

Back in March 1970 I received a letter from a former beau, Henry (Sandy) Bertrand, who was *president-director général* of Les Editions Condé Nast, the Paris publishers of French *Vogue* and *Maison et Jardin*:

> My darling Sheila
> This is my last letter on Condé Nast letterhead—it is a very sad moment for me and letters like yours make it even more difficult to leave. Your affection and support have been so important for me all these years! I will be thinking of you a lot and I hope that you will always let me know when you come to Paris or to London ... and who knows I may be going to Australia one of these days.
>
> I know there have been rough moments for you and there will be more but I have full confidence that you will come through with flying colours.

Best luck, my Sheila, and let's keep in touch.
All my love
Sandy

With the Newhouse family ownership of Condé Nast, there were, I suppose one could say, expected changes or redundancies, both editorial and managerial, among the staff who had been appointed by the president, Iva Patcevitch, in all the *Vogues*. (I was to be one, as you will have read.) Sandy and I had been friends for a very long time, way back since the early 1950s. During part of that time we had a rather special romance one summer in the South of France at Saint Tropez. It was never going to be permanent. He was *the* most stunningly handsome, charming heterosexual bachelor in France at the time. I was only one of many willing conquests!

It may amuse you to know that when we first met I was a blonde, having that very day allowed the famous Parisian hairdresser Antoine to persuade me to let him change the colour of my then mousey-brown hair. In those days there were not the subtle colourings or tintings of today—one could choose blonde, dyed black or henna red. Stupidly I risked being bleached. The result was just awful. Because, as they explained, my hair had shades of red in it (I was born with strawberry blonde curls) the wretched peroxide or whatever they used turned me into a horrible brassy blonde. I simply hated the way I looked, although others seemed to like it. I later made Antoine change it back, even though he told me that I was starting to go grey. (All the women in my family on my mother's side started going grey in their thirties—luckily a pleasant shade of greyish white, I mean white-ish grey, not pepper and salt, nor with nasty yellowish tones, as we have all been non-smokers.)

I think it was Maurice Chevalier who said 'Many a man has fallen in love with a girl in a light so dim he would not have chosen a suit in it.' It so happened that Frank Tubbs (the fashion buyer from Myer's London Office) and I were dining together in a fairly dimly lit restaurant when this tall attractive Frenchman came over to our table and introduced himself. Yes, the liaison started with what is commonly called a pick-up. Previously Tubby (as I called him) had said to me 'Don't look round but there is a man who has been staring at you all through dinner.' For some people it may well be true that 'blondes have more fun'. But in my experience the real fun began when I was no longer a blonde—or shall we say when I was a temporary one—in a dimly lit restaurant.

When I was living in Sydney and working with Vogue, there were other 'liaisons'—I hasten to say never more than one at a time, and discounting the odd illicit flirtation (never with a married man). During a ten-day *Vogue* Australia fashion promotion in Japan, I met up with an old friend Brian Murray, then the naval attaché to our embassy in Tokyo. He was my distinguished escort to a few official receptions and we enjoyed each other's company. When he returned to live in Canberra, we became lovers. He was a widower, with three small children. I definitely did not consider myself stepmother material, and to be honest neither did Brian. We enjoyed weekends together, mainly in my apartment in Point Piper, went sailing on the harbour, and dined with other friends or à deux at 39 Wolseley Road.

After about six months the sexual relationship ended but we remained firm friends. I knew he was looking for a wife, and he soon met someone he considered suitable. When he told me who the intended was, I tried my hardest to advise against this second marriage in a hurry, as I felt he was being tricked into it. Sadly he later admitted it was 'a terrible mistake' and that 'the union was never consummated' and that they had agreed to divorce. Happily, after some time he was to meet the perfect woman for him and to marry her. Together, Brian Murray and Janette Paris, a former school teaching nun, became enthusiastic winemakers on their Doonkuna Estate outside Canberra.

Perhaps you can imagine my amazement when I heard in 1982 that Brian was to be appointed the Governor of Victoria. I was now living in Melbourne and the next time we met I had to curtsey to His Excellency! The Queen, meantime, had made him a Knight and I met Jan for the first time as Lady Murray. I loved her immediately, as most people I know do. They made an ideal couple and were possibly the most popular occupiers of Government House for many years. Their patronage at any fundraising event guaranteed good ticket sales. I was among their list of personal chums who were included in some of the formal and informal dinners and receptions. We (about ten of us, which included his sister Mary Archer) were devastated when Brian was forced to resign under pressure from the then Premier of Victoria in 1985. Personally I still think that, in doing so, John Cain made a grave error that lost him a few marks. We, the FOMs (friends of the Murrays), used to dine together regularly once a month, with Brian and Jan joining us when they came to Melbourne. Alas, Brian's health suddenly deteriorated and he died from cancer aged only sixty-nine. He was given a state funeral with full naval honours in St Paul's Cathedral in Melbourne on 12 June 1991. Together with literally thousands of others, I attended to farewell Rear-Admiral Sir Brian Stewart Murray KCMG AO, this man who had served his country and particularly the State of Victoria with such distinction.

**6**

We lay aside letters never to read
them again, and at last destroy
them out of discretion, and so
disappears the most beautiful,
the most immediate breath of life,
irrecoverably for ourselves and
for others.

**Goethe**

# A Mixed Salad of Letters

Like most people, I have destroyed many many letters, but happily have kept more than a few. Some are important to me, some are interesting, some nice, some nasty. Some were written to me and some are copies of those written by me to others. I value all of them as a record, but have often wondered how to co-ordinate them in such a way that they might make interesting reading for others.

I finally decided to copy the idea used in one of my favourite books, *Nehru's Letters to His Sister*. Written mostly while Nehru was in prison in India between about 1930 and 1955, and all to the same person (his sister Betty), they were published in chronological order. At the end of each letter (like a sort of postscript) personal or historical notes were added by another of Nehru's sisters, Krishna Nehru Hutheesing.

I hope you will forgive me, but my mixed salad of letters is haphazard time-wise and ignores any protocol as to which writers might be considered more important than others. I shall start with one from my brother Colonel Guy Scotter, written to me from London on 14 February 1981 after he had attended the funeral of our cousin General Sir William Scotter KCB OBE MC, who died suddenly just before he was to go to Brussels as Deputy Supreme Allied Commander Europe.

Dear Sheila

Enclosed are the order of service for Bill's funeral and the obituaries about him—Times and Telegraph. It was a wonderful funeral with about 20 generals there, including the full Army Board, and many senior officers from Germany, USA, Canada, France and other Commonwealth countries. It was held in the Royal Garrison Church in Aldershot and the congregation was about 600 strong. The pall bearers were provided by the Border Regiment as was the band that played during the service. The Gurkhas were also there. The Queen was represented and Field Marshall Carver came. It was a fine crisp day with brilliant sunshine and all in all it was very moving. Jean and family were magnificent. Such a sad thing ... Lots of people asked after you at the funeral. All love Guy

Written from London on the same day in 1981 was a letter from Bill's wife (well, now widow) Jean:

Dearest Sheila

This won't be a proper letter, only to say thank you for telephoning and writing and for the <u>lovely</u> flowers, which brought you in amongst us on Bill's SHINING marvellous funeral day.

No, nobody suspected heart trouble. They kept telling him his BP was like a 25 year old's. But he did have these rings round his irises. I often wondered. Am not <u>at ALL</u> bitter, funny, and I only hope this doesn't come later, the magazine articles all say one is supposed to be ... I always knew he was on loan, from the first brush with cancer in the late 50s, and each week a bonus after that. Whenever he had a gyppy tummy my heart contracted secretly and I thought this is it ...

Am so grateful he had the 2 years of proper soldiering in Germany, with all the feedback and the glory, after so many years on the staff treadmill in shiny trousers at MOD. Do wish you'd been able to come and see your pictures much admired on the stairs. Am going to ask Guy to DO something with these when the luggage gets back from SHAPE soon.

And most grateful of all I am for the last 3 months in our comic super wee flat on the river. We lived like two hippies, no hassles except ... 'had we done our French homework?' and no other stress at all to make us snappy with each other. I was so happy and most comforting thing of all I did keep saying so. Haven't been able to write this sort of soppy stuff to other people, though the children know it and are glad too. The mail is overwhelming. So many people adored our darling Bill.

It was super to get your news—too long without it ...

I have put your phone number in the book and who knows, though Australia is too new ground for me to think of breaking, you were sweet to invite me though, good to look forward. Would be more likely to go west first, old ground ...

But for now I must stay put and grin until I can bear it.

Tons of love
Jean

PS [...] Did you know we finally did go on a long lovely Swan's Hellenic Cruise last summer. What luck. Bill <u>adored</u> it, lots of little mountains to be first up as well as sun and much 'culchah'.

Both letters about Bill's funeral arrived in Melbourne together. My adored brother Guy and I were regular letter writers to each other. Since childhood we had written to our parents in India every single week, so the habit stuck. I miss writing to Guy dreadfully—he died in January 1987. I try to keep up the writing practice with gentle Penny Scotter, my sister-in-law, who was such a wonderful wife to Guy. She now lives in one of those picturesque little houses right in the heart of Lymington, Hampshire (UK). However, I have to confess that I am often inclined to use the telephone—we both enjoy chatting.

I still keep in touch with my energetic cousin-in-law Jean, who comes from a large Scottish family. Three of her four brothers were priests and her father was a Doctor of Divinity. Lady Scotter holds a Bachelor of Arts degree in classics (ex-Girton College, Cambridge) and her interests are theatre, opera, ballet, fine sewing and reading—exactly my own interests, with the exception of sewing. I'm simply hopeless at sewing of any kind, let alone 'fine'.

From Dame Zara Holt
*18 Millicent Avenue, Toorak 3142*
*27 June 1971*

Darling Sheila
This is just a keep-in-touch letter and to tell you how
thrilled I am that you have landed such an important
and fascinating job. I am absolutely furious the other
idea did not come off, but they are a bunch of nongs
and certainly do not deserve the best.

   I cannot tell you how everyone regrets that Australia
has lost you and how much all your many friends will
miss you. I myself really grieve that you are no longer
in Sydney.
All my love
Zara

This letter was written after Dame Zara heard that I had
accepted a job with the Revlon Corporation and would soon
be leaving for New York. Sorry, I am not going to identify the
'nongs' she mentioned as, believe it or not, after all these
years they are still around and in my opinion deserve the
description.

From Gordon Chater
*The Comedy Theatre, Melbourne*
*Saturday*

Sheila dear,
Last night was the Best Night in Melbourne—your incomparable Self, Home Cooking, Laughter, Warmth—and that most touching (for me) moment when you said you'd like me for a brother! Felt very wanted and special then. It was wonderful of Des to drive me home—what a distinguished man. The whole evening was as rounded and perfect as one could ever wish for. Thank you.

And I hope we'll see each other again v. soon.
Much love
Gordie

Gordon Chater is not only one of my favourite actors, but definitely one of my favourite men. And yes I would have liked him to have been my brother. Actually he is one of the people who encouraged me to write this book when I attended the Melbourne launch of *his* fascinating and amusing (natch!) autobiography called *(The Almost Late) Gordon Chater.* Des was Desmond Daly, a very close friend at the time.

---

From Maina Gielgud, Artistic Director of the Australian Ballet
*15 December 1993*

Dear Sheila
So many thanks for your lovely fax—yes it is good to
know there are people who understand and support—it
means a great deal to me to hear it from you.
Very much love
Maina

My fax of 10 December 1993 had said:

Just to let you know you have the strongest support
and admiration from thousands of friends for all you
have done for the Australian Ballet ... I am one ... and
happy to stand and be counted if needed ... I mean
this! Even elegant tall poppies don't escape the Aussie
knockers it seems ...
Bon courage and love
Sheila Scotter

This was a stressful period for Maina. The Australian Ballet
Board were asking for her resignation and the press were having a field day. A full account of those turbulent times in John
Larkin's biography *Maina Gielgud* makes for intriguing reading ... well, it did for me!

From Patricia Tuckwell
*121 Hamilton Terrace, London NW8*
*6 July 1964*

Darling Sheila
Just a note to tell you that yesterday I was safely
delivered of a 9lb son! So like his Dad that it makes
you burst out laughing. I did try to have him too soon
and spent most of the last months in bed, but we are
all three very well indeed, George even having survived
being present and holding my hand throughout, which
was really wonderful.

He is called Mark Hubert (the latter is one of
George's names) and we are delighted with him.
Much love
Patricia

It was such a happy relief to receive this letter and to know
that all was well. Patricia and I had been friends for many
years since the late 1950s when, as Bambi Shmith, she had
been one of Australia's most elegant models and we had
worked together in Sydney. She helped me organise the
Marketing Division for Everglaze and Banlon in Australia and
New Zealand for Joseph Bancroft of Wilmington, Delaware,
USA. During a trip overseas she met her beloved George (Earl
of Harewood). Theirs was a true love story and they eventually married but for a few years there were frustrating times
when they needed discreet friends. I am glad I was one.

George Harewood must be credited with a major contribution to the progress of opera in Australia. He later

became our overseas director on the first Board of the Australian Opera. (I had privately telephoned him on behalf of the chairman, Claude Alcorso.) Not only did his name and reputation add enormous strength to our small Board, but his experience and invaluable advice were always available for us. In 1980, when I was appointed to the board of the Victoria State Opera in Melbourne, I again asked a favour. Would he consider being our president? Yes, he would—and he accepted, again becoming available for much-needed advice. I think that both opera companies have a great deal to thank Patricia for. Could they have got Lord Harewood if Patricia Tuckwell had been an American, for example?

---

From Sophie Mackenzie-Charrington
*St Georges School*
*Ascot*
*Berkshire SL5 7DZ*
*6 February 1997*

Dear Mrs Scotter
I am a final year student completing A levels at
St Georges Ascot. As part of my History of Art course
I am required to write a dissertation on a chosen topic.
I am particularly interested in post war fashion. My
mother suggested I contact you as I require some first
hand information.
    My dissertation will explore the reasons why styles
appear and re-appear. I would appreciate your help and

enclose a short questionnaire which I hope you will find time to complete.

Yours sincerely

Sophie Mackenzie-Charrington

*1 After the war came the New Look, which was a powerful trend. Do you think this still influences fashion today—if so how?*

My typed answer:

Unfortunately I do not think The New Look influences fashion today. I only wish it did. In 1945 Christian Dior knew that women were fed up with square shouldered rather mannish jackets with skimpy straight tight shorter skirts (due to the wartime shortage of good fabrics). We all <u>loved</u> Dior's wide swirling pleated and full skirts, neat cinched-in waists, feminine necklines and long tight sleeves. I was a model in London then and wore these divine clothes! Perhaps the lingerie designers of today are influenced by Dior's revolutionary New Look ... there are now pretty corselets with lots of lace, very tiny waists, very sexy boned under-bras on the market.

*2 Do you think that fashion is a cycle and trends that just keep on reappearing?*

My answer:

Fashion used to come in cycles in the old days ... influenced by the courts and nobles of the period. Today I think most young designers of ready-to-wear are influenced more by Show Business ... rock stars, film stars, and dare I say it, famous drag queens, transvestites, you name it. Occasionally elegance is copied or inspires … eg 'My Fair Lady' and 'Coco' etc. I think the magazines have a lot to do with this … there is very little real leadership or more important still '<u>guidance</u>'.

*3 Why is the style of the 40s's still being used today?*
My answer:

I am sorry I cannot answer this adequately for you as I do not agree that the style of the '40s is around today in strength … unless one counts the more military belted coats and jackets, nautical gold braids on sleeves etc. and boots. The decade of the '40s should in any case be divided. The boring wartime fashion from 1940 to 1945 … then after that Christian Dior completely changed the look and shape from 1945 to 1950.'

I then wrote by hand: 'Sophie … I hope this is helpful and wish you luck in your A levels … one tip for future years, always *sign* your letters … SS. 16 February 1997.' (She had omitted to sign her letter to me, leaving her printed name only.)

Obviously no offence was taken. Perhaps, like me, Sophie does not resent constructive criticism as she wrote back immediately saying, 'Thank you so much for completing the questionnaire for me. It will be very important in the conclusion of my project. I am sorry about forgetting to sign my letter. Thank you for the tip. SOPHIE MACKENZIE-CHARRINGTON'—this time, signed with a flourish in bold handwriting.

From Rex Harrison
*The Ritz*
*Piccadilly*
*London W1V 9DG*

Darling Sheila

Your lovely green note arrived safely. You are wasted on that huge brown continent. Why don't you come back and decorate Mayfair properly? God knows it needs it!!

W ... is still skulking around in a huge black overcoat looking very sinister and un-doctor-like!

I have to keep explaining to the English that he is not really a doctor of the 'Help, Help' variety but <u>another</u> kind.

Much love to you all. Don't repeat my jokes in this letter to Mrs W—they are <u>kindly</u> meant.

With much love to you

Rex

I am not going to identify W ... except to say that he is a good friend of mine who happened to be over in London at the time Rex was celebrating his eightieth birthday. Both he and his wife and children had been very hospitable to Rex Harrison while he was in Australia. He loved them all. As for me leaving this 'huge brown continent' ... I told him 'No way—Professor Higgins.'

An air letter from Sir Francis Chichester written on board
MV *Port Nelson* on passage to New Zealand
   *7 February 1968*

Dear Sheila

I hope it is not too late to thank you for those lovely
flowers you sent me at the Naval Hospital last year and
your tender enquiry for my screw driver. I badly needed
that same tool later in the year when I began to fear
getting a screw loose. I read that Amy Johnson's doctor
told her four months after her flight to Australia that
she was on the verge of insanity.

   Anyway, my health packed up under the strain of
land-worries and people-pressure and each ailment was
worse than the last till it bolted on this lazy sea-trip
which is setting us up again (Sheila, my Sheila—took a
pounding last year too). This is my apology for not
writing to you sooner—coupled with the fact that I
originally thought Sheila Scott had sent me the flowers
because she wrote to me the same day. Anyway, I hope
we shall meet again when we visit Sydney after NZ.
My Sheila sends you her best wishes to which I add
mine with affection entwined.
Francis

During his solo circumnavigation of the world aboard *Gypsy
Moth IV* Francis put in to Sydney harbour where his beloved
yacht was refitted. I met him and Sheila Chichester through
mutual chums, Hugh and Bar Eaton of Vaucluse, who had
them as house guests.

A few of us all rallied round to help with home cooking and entertaining. I had a small dinner party at home in Point Piper, racking my brains as to what to cook. Both Sheila and Francis were strict vegetarians. Cauliflower au gratin was about all I could come up with then ... nowadays there are masses of more tasty recipes for vegetarian dishes, possibly because there are so many more committed vegetarians, but as I am not one of them (thank goodness), they are not among my vast collection of cookbooks. The meal went well. They were an unusual but intriguing couple to get to know. Francis, I discovered, was a flirt. No, he was not to become one of my 'liaisons' but I certainly enjoyed flirting with him. He told me that I reminded him of Sheila Scott (the famous solo pilot) of whom I gathered he was extremely fond.

After New Zealand in 1968, the Chichesters came back to Sydney to promote Francis's book *Gypsy Moth Circles the World*. He came to dine again at home. I had bought a special leather-bound edition numbered and signed by the author, and limited to 500, of which my copy was 382. Francis insisted on signing it twice, adding 'Dear Sheila, I have looked forward a year to this delightful evening at Flat 2, 39 Wolseley Road Point Piper Sydney 8.3.68.'

In pre-fax days opening a telegram from overseas was usually exciting. During the 1980s I received a few from one of my favourite artists, an Australian who resided in Italy and returned to Melbourne about every two years. The message was always the same:

LUNCH PLEASE FRIDAY 16 OCTOBER USUAL PLACE USUAL
TIME
UNUSUAL LOVE
SMART

The usual place was upstairs at The Florentino, at the table in the window; the time, one o'clock; and the unusual love was from Jeffrey Smart. Both being punctual people we always arrived at the exact time and caught up with the latest 'goss' over an always perfectly delicious meal.

As a context for the 'unusual' love, I recommend Jeffrey's 1996 autobiography *Not Quite Straight*, my copy of which he signed 'With lots of love to my darling Sheila. No substitute for old beloved friends. As ever Jeffrey'.

---

*Ambassade de France en Australie*
*Canberra*
*4 January 1994*

Dear, dear Sheila
I wouldn't let the year start without telling you how happy I am to know that such people, such women, as you do exist on earth and give it the touch of elegance, charm and wit without which life on it would be drab, colourless and frankly uninteresting.

Dieu a créé la femme, et, quand on songe à vous, on sait qu'il a eu raison!

I am soon to retire and time is [nearing?—unclear]

for me, but my most heartfelt wish is to see you as often as I can before I leave Australia.

Please accept, dear Sheila, all my wishes and that small present which tells of places and times very dear to me. Avec mon hommage le plus affectueux
Philippe

Philippe Baude was an extremely popular ambassador. I was not the only person to miss him dreadfully when he retired. He has since married a charming New Zealander, Jeanette, and together they spend a great part of the year in Auckland. During their visits to Melbourne we all enjoy happy moments together with mutual French and Australian friends ... *Vive l'entente cordiale!*

---

From Lady Murray
*Government House*
*Melbourne 3004*
*27 July 1982*

Dear Sheila
We spent the happiest evening with you last week, and Brian and I want to thank you most warmly.

A lovely fire, your delicious 'bangers and mash', and very special company made a lovely occasion.

We hope you enjoy this bottle of wine and look forward to seeing you again soon.
Fondest regards from
Jan Murray

**Above left:** With Alan Stockdale, who was then Victoria's shadow treasurer when The Lord's Taverners played the 500 Club of the Liberal Party at the Cope Williams Vineyard in Romsey, Victoria. **Above right:** Two opening batsmen for The Taverners—John Lill (now president of the Victorian Branch) and John MacKinnon (now chairman of the New South Wales Branch). **Below left:** At another fundraising day for The Lord's Taverners and the Variety Club, at Red Hill, Victoria, with Greg Chappell. **Below right:** Elizabeth Proust, who was Guest Speaker at a Taverners lunch at the top of the Rialto and who is as keen on cricket as I am.

**Above:** The Lord's Taverners' Annual General Meeting is traditionally held at the Hilton on the Park in Melbourne, followed by a well-attended cocktail party in the Delacombe Room. I am flanked by Dr John Lill (our president) and Victorian cricketer Nigel Murch.
**Below:** As team manager at another charity match in Romsey I insisted on being included in this group shot (I am the one with long hair) and will be unpopular with some for naming only three Taverners gentlemen in the centre of the front row: 'Typhoon' Tyson (captain) flanked on his right by, Andrew Buckle (now national chairman) and, on his left, by Gordon Cope Williams, owner of this enchanting cricket ground and pavilion in Romsey.

Above left: In France with Claude Alcorso … We enjoyed a special liaison way back in the 50s and I have remained an admirer. Above right: In my apartment in Paris with photographer Helmut Newton below an oil painting by Mary Talbot. Below left: My short hair period—and starting to go grey. (Photo Geoffrey Lee) Below right: Entering Maxim's restaurant in Paris with Sandy Bertrand who was the French head of Condé Nast, publishers of French *Vogue* and *Maison et Jardin*.

**Above left:** Showing only the top half of my super-duper mink coat, photographed in my apartment in Paris by that genius Helmut Newton just before he became world famous. **Above right:** Yours truly as a photographer who never became famous. **Below left:** Arriving at Tokyo Airport for *Vogue*'s fashion and travel promotion in Japan 1968, all dressed alike. (Top) model Elizabeth Ford, (centre) fashion editor Patricia dos Remedios, and myself—photographed by David Hewison who came with us but did not dress alike. **Below right:** Daniel Salem, the international vice-president of Condé Nast Publications, in my office at 49 Clarence Street, Sydney.

**Above:** A group shot by David Hewison of the editorial staff of *Vogue* Australia in the 1960s. Back row, left to right: Suzanne Gartner, Judy Cook, Elizabeth Reeve, Jo Ann Fuller, me, Diana Crowther, Annie Hockey, Eve Harman. On floor, left to right: Trish Hurst, Susie Edenborough, Victoria Alexander. (Photo courtesy of *Vogue*) **Below:** As editor of *Vogue* I worked from a round table rather than a desk. All planning meetings were held here, which definitely eliminated strife over precedence! Moreover, it was used for a good many informal working lunches ... sometimes even for formal ones.

**Above:** On my return from Europe I was asked to announce Australia's best dressed men for *Mode* magazine … Left to right: the late John Bell, Stuart Membery, Trent Nathan, George Gross, Robert Burton, me, Judge Jim McClelland, 'Snow' Swift, David McNicoll and Peter Janson. Date: Early 80s. **Left:** Entering the Carita Salon, 11 Faubourg St Honoré in Paris, 1969, to have my hair re-styled. I really loved that mink coat by Alixandre of New York, and thought about eventually using the skins to line a raincoat ... but in the end (after many years) gave it to a friend who lives and winters in Europe. (Photo courtesy of *Vogue*)

**Above left:** At a drinks party I gave for Robert Carrier (left), photographed with Leo Schofield in my apartment by another guest, Bob Hart. **Above right:** At the Park Hyatt, Sydney, 2 December 1991, at the gala dinner for The Australian Ballet—on my right Alan Jones and on my left Bill Haffenden. **Below left:** Celebrating after a first night at the ballet with (left) Professor Dick Denton and (right) Sir Ian Potter in the Victorian Arts Centre, Melbourne. **Below right:** Derby Day at Flemington, 1995, as guests of Louis Vuitton. I don't think young John MacKinnon approved of us being snapped in front of that sign!

**Above left:** Between Luke and Sam Parker Bowles, the two grandsons of Sir Ian Potter and Mrs Gwen Potter, at lunch in the Park Hyatt, Sydney, in August 1990. **Above right:** Sir Ian Potter, his daughter Carolyn, myself and Carolyn's husband Simon Parker Bowles. **Below left:** Bill Haffenden with the portrait he had commissioned to celebrate my 70th birthday. The artist: Pamela Graevenitz of Scotland. **Below right:** Admirers of and attentive listeners to Leo Schofield, then (1995) Melbourne Festival supremo in the State Theatre of the Victorian Arts Centre. Left to right: Valerie Lawson, Ian Lincoln, myself and Noel Pelly.

Jan's handwritten note was nice to receive and so was the delicious wine from the Murrays' Doonkuna Estate. Some may not approve of serving sausages and mashed potatoes to a governor and his lady. But my theory is that people who are obliged to attend dozens of formal lunches and dinners as part of their job jolly well appreciate really simple food.

---

Part of the will and testament of my long-time and much-loved friend Judy Barraclough Potts, dated 26 June 1969:

> I appoint James K Walker of Colebrook Springvale in the State of New South Wales and Sheila Scotter of Sydney in the State of New South Wales, Executor Executrix and Trustees of this my Will and Guardians of my infant children but in case of the death of either of my said Trustees then I empower the survivor of them to so act.

Judy Barraclough, in her time, was without doubt the most elegant high-fashion model in the country. She also modelled for the London couturier Norman Hartnell while her surgeon husband Ian was studying for his fellowship of the Royal College of Surgeons in the UK. Thank goodness she is still with us and living in Potts Point (not named after the family!) and that will is no longer valid. Her two sons are both successful men with children of their own—Anthony a well-known photographer and director of television commercials in Sydney, and Timothy the director of the National Gallery of Victoria in Melbourne. Judy still calls me their godmother.

When I left Australia for London to become director of Revlon's Ultima division, inevitably I had to resign from the Board of the Australian Opera. I was sad to leave them but flattered by the charming letter from the chairman, Claude Alcorso, written on 26 January 1972:

Dear Sheila

On behalf of our colleagues I should like to tell you how deeply sorry we are about your resignation from the Board because of your departure from Australia.

You have been a Foundation Director and have made an outstanding contribution to the progress we have made. We sincerely hope that it will be possible for you to return to Australia for the Opening Festival at the new Sydney Opera House next year as, if we shall perform to the standards we hope to achieve, this will be due to no small extent to your efforts.

My colleagues and I would hope that you will remain in touch with the company and consider yourself as an 'Ambassador at Large' for us. You know our policy and I have given instructions that you will continue to be informed of our activities.

It is with great personal sadness that I say farewell and best wishes in your new activities.

Yours sincerely

Claudio

Having observed the progress of this exciting young opera

company, it gives me a nice warm feeling to remember that I was a foundation director. Now, a quarter of a century later, I am still a great fan and proud to be one of their patrons and on the National Council of Opera Australia.

---

When living in London at 73 St James's Street, I received the following letter from the tenant of a flat in the same block, but on the floor below, who had a lot of late night visitors and jolly noisy parties in the early hours of the morning. The letter was written on 6 October:

> Dear Miss Scotter
> I understand you have complained yet again. I would like to point out to you that my windows were shut last night. I would also like to point out that I pay the rent and rates for my premises and if, as I was, I wish to entertain my son on his return from New York on my own premises I shall continue to do so.
> I will not have you dictate my terms of living here and should you make another attempt I shall complain to the management for harassment.
> Yours truly
> Sandy Fawkes

I wrote back on 7 October 1978:

> Dear Mrs Fawkes
> Oh dear what an aggressive letter you wrote! Please be

assured I simply <u>loathe</u> complaining and only do so when kept awake in the middle of the night (and not every time I hasten to add). Luckily I am a heavy sleeper and only loud noise wakes me, but <u>un</u>luckily I am the sort of journalist whose writing suffers considerably after broken sleep, and writing is my livelihood.

Thank you for closing your windows when you have a late party, but very often it is the loud bang of your front door and sometimes rather loud shouting before you do so that wakens me initially. I'm sure you wouldn't be inconsiderate of others on purpose and are probably unaware of how noisy voices sound at 0230 hours in this old and by no means soundproof building.

I should welcome your talking to the Management or Landlords whom I'm sure would check the facts with the night porter ... and even explain a certain clause in all our leases. But perhaps two talented women could be more neighbourly and get together over a drink or a coffee and air our problems, I should welcome this at any time except between 11 o'clock at night and 9 in the morning! How about it?
Very sincerely yours
Sheila Scotter

It did the trick! I received a reply on 14 October:

Dear Miss Scotter
What a nice civilised letter, thank you.

Thank you, too, for the raffle tickets which I have sent off with all fingers crossed. I should love to have a drink with you sometime, could we make it early in November as I am frantically finishing my next book and have to do the provinces next week exploiting the last one in paperback. Also, I am off to Australia in February next year to launch [a book] out there and would love to talk to you about the places I should see whilst I am there. I am really very excited about the trip and don't want to miss a thing.

Looking forward to meeting you
Yours sincerely
Sandy Fawkes

---

From Dame Elisabeth Murdoch
*3 December 1996*

Dearest Sheila
Congratulations on a wonderful party last night! Thank you most warmly for seating me at your table and belated thanks for faxing me those with whom I would be sitting [...]

I enjoyed talking with all my companions and so pleased to meet Geoffrey Court, whose parents I admire and like immensely. Sad that his mother died— far too young.

I was lost in admiration for your organisation of everything from the programme of entertainment to all those fantastic prizes. I do hope the financial result was up to expectations.

Many many happy returns … you looked superb last night and you must have felt rewarded by yet another great success.

Again thanking you for looking after me so well.
Affectionately
Elisabeth

Dame Elisabeth is renowned for writing her thank you letters the day after the event—always handwritten and never just 'thanks for a lovely evening' on a postcard. The party in this case was a gala dinner on 2 December 1996 to raise dollars for the Australian Opera (now Opera Australia). Held in the Mayfair Ballroom of the Grand Hyatt, Melbourne, it raised over $61,000. I must clarify that I was *joint* chairman with my friend Heather Lustig. We had a wonderfully helpful committee and terrific co-operation from the Hyatt staff. As I always say 'People are only as good as their brief' and Heather and I are pretty good with our briefs!

The parents Elisabeth refers to in her letter were Sir Charles and Lady Court of Western Australia. And others at my table to whom she enjoyed talking were Ivan and Mary Ellen Deveson, John and Christina Stitt, Patrick Griffin and Robert and Sara McKay.

From Diane Masters, a great supporter and fundraiser for the
Victorian College of the Arts
> *6 May 1996*

> Dear Sheila
> One of the Friends of the VCA, Jim Darby, specially took
> these photographs for you—of me and Clive Gregory
> (Deputy Director of VCA) and President of the Friends
> (Canon Albert McPherson) at our Cocktail Party with
> Guest Speaker Maurice Scott—when Lawrie Carew
> arranged display of Red Dress and Accessories on stage as
> a lovely splash of colour against the black backdrop with
> the ubiquitous Silver Stars—and I encouraged audience
> members to follow your example and donate gowns etc to
> VCA wardrobe to help young Opera Singers involved in
> special performances, auditions etc Thanks again [...]
> Diane

This now rather famous 'red dress', which I mentioned earlier,
was designed by the Australian designer John Cavill. It was a
gorgeous true red (not bluey red nor orangey red) *peau-de-soie*
with long sleeves and a lovely collar, cinched in at the waist,
with a fullish skirt that was slightly longer at the back than at
the front (the back was floor length). Shoes and ankles were
always on view, which meant I had to buy red pantyhose and
get some of those satin 'bridal' court shoes dyed to match. I
borrowed a ruby-and-gold necklace with matching earrings,
from John Batterby of Melee Jewellers, and Doreen Levine
(Cavill's top couture dressmaker) made me a sensibly sized
clutch bag in matching material.

I loved everything but have not worn the dress or the accessories since the night of 2 December 1990. Shame on me, so many might say, but after all my long years in black and white, I just did not like myself in red. However, I do own a dress in black taffeta in the same style, which Cavill kindly agreed to repeat exactly. It is still in my wardrobe and comes out quite frequently (so it won't be going to the VCA, Diane, *until* I die!)

I have donated other garments since the red dress and do believe we should help young students obtain something suitable for auditions or important appearances without having to spend a fortune. Theatre companies, also, are grateful for certain items (best to check first). I gave Playbox at The Malthouse two fur coats and a silver fox fur which they could cut up and do what they liked with. And the head of the millinery department in the Australian Ballet (the genius Kevin Regan) is always grateful for good hats, jewellery and unusual trimmings, feather fans and so on.

---

From John Greer
*New Zealand*
*16 January 1983*

Dear Sheila
It had to happen. On the very first morning it started.

"Don't use that for the butter ... Oh God isn't there a sharp knife? ... What—no bloody castor sugar ... You must have had that for 3 months."

And then a lesson on how to make mustard. The correct way to dry lettuce. And—dear Christ—the right way to eat a peach (very Dame Edna that one).

"Clean that, don't wash that, don't touch this. Not here—there, oh God don't be so stupid."

A litany of do's and dont's—unceasing! Extraordinary behaviour. The officiousness and bossiness in somebody else's house. The continual striving for supremacy, top dog, boss.

One simply has to assume that you have an entourage of sycophants who—so that they can be associated with and bask in the ambience of S.S.—will suffer any insult, any put down, with the result that your native imperiousness is exacerbated—compounded.

Obviously our relationship had no solid basis of mutual esteem or appreciation.

Of course on my side there was the aesthetic appreciation for the great style, the instinctive elegance—Ca Va [sic] sans dire—but even the chic of Araby is not enough ...

I regret that my forbearance—which was considerable—ran out.

The above will, no doubt, be the cause of deathless offence—but it had to be said.

Nevertheless I wish you a Happy and prosperous New Year and all thats best for the future.

John

P. S. Richard totally dissociates himself from this. According to him I have overreacted. Since he refuses to be involved—Sagittarian solidarity??—had to find a professional typist. Fell the other day and sprained my right arm. Its hell to write.

Oh dear! This was a shocker of a letter to receive. John Greer, an Irish-very-Irish-New Zealander, had been one of the men in my life for umpteen years ... like about twenty-five. When one travels to New Zealand (or to anywhere else for that matter) it is a cosy feeling to know that you have a romantic 'liaison' there. I used to fly over to Auckland quite often and always stayed in his stylish 'glass pavilion' house high up in the Waitakere Ranges. His invitations were always 'Stay as long as you like as long as you do the cooking'—both of which I did. He was not much good in the kitchen department and I'll admit there were sometimes a few 'words' between us because I could never find a really sharp knife or found he had made lumpy mustard and so on. And yes, I have to confess to being a bit bossy ... but only in the kitchen ... yet I have never been able to fathom why his usually controlled Irish temper flared up this particular time. I absolutely agree with Richard (Frith), a close chum to both of us and whose birthday is the day after mine, that Greer had most definitely over-reacted. I was furious and was about to pick up the telephone, then decided against it. Instead I went out and bought one of those bad taste 'In Sympathy' cards. Inside were the words 'My deepest thoughts are with you in your tragic loss'. I left it unsigned, but addressed the envelope in my own handwriting.

To my utter amazement I recently picked up the telephone (in June 1997) and a familiar Irish voice said 'Is this Miss Sheila Scotter?' Immediately recognising his voice I answered 'Yes it is, John Greer.' We had not spoken for years and frankly I wondered whether he was still alive. Rather bluntly, I asked, 'How old are you?' He was ninety-two.

Apparently he had seen me on television in Auckland and decided to get my telephone number and call. 'You looked bloody marvellous and it brought back memories of the past.' I warned him I was writing a book on certain aspects of my life and had already included that letter he wrote in 1983. 'Oh darling you can't put that in, give me your address and I'll write you another.' I sent him a copy of a magazine in which my apartment in Albert Park was featured, plus some amusing press clippings and a recent photograph. On 20 June he wrote:

Dear Sheila
When I saw you briefly on TV the other night
something extraordinary happened. I simply couldn't
get to sleep that night. So I decided to get in touch. (I've
always been in love with you I guess.) The memories of
happy times came crowding back and I wanted to hear
that lovely voice again. It was exciting to stay with you
in Sydney and great to have you visit me.

You can imagine how heartbreaking it was to sell
that super house but I had no choice—I could no
longer drive a car. I miss that million dollar view.
However I am reasonably contented here. Actually it is
a very special retirement village and I have an attractive

apartment overlooking a farm—lots of green fields and trees. I've just finished reading the magazine and your letter. Your flat looks marvellous and you look as elegant as ever. I'm very impressed by your sculptures and pictures, and by the fact that you're still very active and switched on (that expression dates me).

Considering I'm 92 I keep reasonably well. But I do suffer from 'Menière's disease' which affects my balance. Trust me to have a disability with a glamorous French name and for which there is no medication. I think I first met you around 1954 when you would be about 30. I'm glad you keep in such good health. Fortunately my eyes are very good so I still read a lot. I'd be miserable without books.

I can't wait to read your memoirs. When will it be published? I shall certainly send for a copy.
Fondest love dear Sheila
John

From Barry Humphries (written on a flight between Singapore and London)
*28 February 1987*

DEAREST SHEILA, WHAT A NERVE!
A PROMPTER 'THANK YOU' YOU DESERVE,
I MUST SEEM AN UNGRATEFUL KNAVE
TO SHUN THOSE GIFTS YOU KINDLY GAVE
WHEN I PERFORMED MY SHOW IN MELBOURNE

PROVING THAT I WAS LESS THAN WELL-BORN!
SO NOW, MONTHS LATER, I AGAIN
TAKE OUT MY LEAKIN' FOUNTAIN PEN
WITH DOGGEREL THAT'S LESS THAN CLEVER
AND THANKS THAT'S BETTER LATE THAN NEVER.
SOON, MELBOURNE-BOUND, MY JOURNEY WENDS
THEN MAY I, SHEILA, MAKE AMENDS?
Fondly
Barry

As far as I'm concerned Barry Humphries can make amends any time he likes and as often as he likes. I've been a fan of his for umpteen years and still am. Dame Edna would certainly give him 10 out of 10 for manners ... his thank you notes are always handwritten. This one was for a few bottles of a new (then) 'Chi' mineral water imported from New Zealand that I had sent to his dressing room on his opening night in the Palace Theatre in St Kilda.

---

From my second husband Alan Ford McIntyre of Melbourne (sent to me in Paris on 25 June 1960)

Dear Sheila
At long last our dopey lawyer got to court on 20 June and the decree becomes absolute in three months from that date.

Surprisingly, to me, neither of us is formally advised by the court; but I'll pick up a copy of the certificate when it becomes available about the end of September, and send it to you.

I am pleased to hear of your raise [in salary] and break in the sun [a holiday in Greece]. As always my best hopes that all goes very well for you.
Alan

Back in those days the Melbourne *Herald* regularly listed divorce decrees. Even though I realised that the name Scotter would not be mentioned (legally it was just McIntyre v. McIntyre), I was still nervous that some smart journo from the gossip or news pages might do a follow-up. So contacted my good friend Pat Jarrett, then the powerful women's editor of a sister daily, the *Sun News Pictorial*, to see whether she would keep an eye on things. Bless her ... she did—mainly because she knew and liked Alan McIntyre very much and was aware of his hatred of publicity of any sort. In fact photographs taken of me at Flemington races or any social 'do' annoyed him intensely, which inevitably became a bone of contention in this marriage.

So it was with great relief that I read a small newspaper clipping and a note from Pat saying 'Quite safe dear. You only rated page 24 right next to the Shipping News and the Tides at Port Phillip Heads and Williamstown! Very few readers dear.'

The clipping read 'Mr Justice Barry has granted the following decrees nisi for divorce in the Supreme Court (June 21st 1960): Alan Ford McIntyre, of Berkeley-St., Hawthorn, from Sheila Winifred Gordon McIntyre formerly of Avenue de Villiers, Paris, France, for desertion.'

From Peter Pagan
    *126 East 30th Street*
    *New York, New York 10016*
    *28 December 1996*

Dearest Sheila

Thank you so much for your fun Christmas card. <u>So</u>
good to hear from you and to know you are *at last*
writing your memoirs. I can only hope that when you
mention our engagement you won't do as Ethel
Merman did in hers. When she came to mention her
marriage with Ernest Borgnine, she started the chapter
by saying she married him—followed by <u>one empty</u>
page!

    I miss not being able to see you but as Rohan has
just gone back to Australia for good (no green card) I
may be out there whilst there's still life—I mean
health—in my body.

    I love you darling and look forward to seeing you
soon.

Yours

Peter

One of my secrets! This engagement to one of Australia's
expatriate actors astonishes a few people in New York and
has certainly raised a few painted eyebrows in certain circles
of Sydney—which amuses us both. I love him, too, but shall
say no more and leave only a *half*-empty page.

From Trent Nathan
*8 February 1994*

Dear Sheila
I really thank you from my heart, you are a wonderful person, your beauty comes from within, that's why you look so beautiful.

Why I was so loud at dinner (and I do apologise to you <u>only</u>, but I did it for a reason) was to <u>really</u> get my point across to MYER MEN while I had them at the dinner table, and it worked!

I will call you when I am in Melbourne, that will be soon I hope!

Thank you my love.
Always
Trent

This was certainly a charming letter to receive from one of my favourite men, the designer Trent Nathan. We had dined long and late together after I had modelled for him when he launched a new sporty-smart-casual line for Myer-Grace Bros in Sydney's Museum of Modern Art. 'Modelled? At seventy-three?' I can hear you say. So I had better explain.

Although there were twelve stunning young professional models, Trent had decided to include some much older 'celebrities' (all friends who loved his clothes), which turned out to be a brilliant idea. Without doubt the absolute star of the evening was Dawn Fraser. As she and I were the oldest, we came on the runway last. The tumultuous applause made us feel that we were as good as any Claudia what's-her-name. Trent had us in black leggings, clunky boots, a classic, beautifully made, long-sleeved white cotton shirt and an elongated black sleeveless gilet. (I still enjoy wearing this outfit.) The show was covered by television news, as well as the national press and glossy magazines. Lawrence Money's 'Spy' column in the *Sunday Age* put an amusing caption to an equally amusing photograph: 'Give the girl a hand. Melbourne ex-model and ex-editor Sheila Scotter, all of 73 years young, returned to the catwalk for the Trent Nathan and Myer-Grace Bros fashion launch in Sydney last week. "If I am 73, that means my legs are only 36 and a half each" argued the Silver Duchess. None dared dispute it.'

From Irene Worth CBE just after she left Australia
*333 West 56th Street*
*NYC 10019*
*14 November 1996*

Dear Sheila
You are the dearest creature. How you cheered me
when you rang at the Regent. They gave me a beautiful
room and were awfully kind. The shock of the city was
tremendous after all the out-back and Bush Country.

I'm reading a very interesting book by Mayse Young
called 'No Place for a Woman'. I wouldn't have 'got' it
before my safari which I <u>adored</u>! I've been very
inspired by my journeys—from the tip of the south to
the top of the north! Melbourne to Darwin! The red
earth, seeing the rivers from the air, rainbow serpent
truly. I bought 4 bark paintings and long to unwrap
when I get home on the 19th. I'm resting a bit at my
sister's house in Santa Monica then to the bedlam of
NY. I rather dread it as I was getting into a beautiful
sense of nature on safari—no telephone and I grilled
some delicious kangaroo at Cooinda Lodge in Kakadu.
The rivers are beautiful and the escarpments took my
breath away. Unforgettable. I'm full of wonder.

What a gift to have your friendship, your kindness,
all wishes
Irene

Irene came back from her safari for an overnight stay at the
Regent Hotel in Sydney before taking off for California and

on to New York where she lives. We had a long chat on the telephone. Later I received this letter—and am pleased to say we still keep in touch, having become good friends during the Melbourne International Festival 1996 when Leo Schofield asked me to take care of this great actress.

My letter on Vogue letterhead
*49 Clarence Street*
*Sydney NSW 2000*
*18 May 1980*

Dear Mr and Mrs Gorton
I wanted to write to tell you how dreadfully sorry I am about the behaviour of one of my guests on Sunday evening at the party you asked me to organise for Monsieur Trudeau.

David McNicoll had given me his solemn word that he would be attending as a private individual and understood perfectly that there was to be no publicity. Therefore the picture and caption published in today's Sydney Daily Telegraph must have caused embarrassment both to you and the Canadian Prime Minister—and may I ask you to pass on my apologies to Monsieur Trudeau.

The evening otherwise was very enjoyable and I loved playing a part in it.
Very sincerely
Sheila Scotter

Before Pierre Trudeau was coming to Australia on a state visit, he had requested a day off in Sydney before meeting our then prime minister John Gorton officially in Canberra. Bettina Gorton asked me to arrange an informal supper party on board the Government's launch (*Captain Phillip*). 'Just with discreet friends,' she emphasised. The date was 17 May which was a Sunday. Trudeau, who was about to face an election in Canada, wanted to go to a night club. Apparently many Canadians at that time (mainly Presbyterians) would not approve of dancing on a Sunday so there was to be no publicity whatsoever. I arranged for about fourteen of us to pick up Pierre and his handsome Mountie from the Admiralty House steps. We toured the harbour while enjoying an informal homemade buffet supper to which all my chums contributed. We later disembarked at Double Bay where hire cars were waiting to take us to the Tabou, the only respectable club I knew that opened on a Sunday. I purposely did not reveal who was in our party when I booked two tables of eight, only implying I had some important French Vogue people with me. I did not even tell Florence and Frank Packer my reason for being unable to dine with them as I usually did on Sundays. As David McNicoll was a good friend and had given me his solemn promise of no publicity, I had included him, but realised in hindsight that this was bloomin' stupid of me.

The moment we got to the Tabou, McNicoll called the *Daily Telegraph* (of which he was then editor-in-chief) and got them to send a photographer. The Mountie and I asked David to leave the party immediately, which he did. I was so angry. The next day, on the front page, was a large shot of Trudeau dancing with Bo-Bo Faulkner, the caption 'Trudeau's

Party at Nightclub' plus a description of the evening ... the whole number.

The Gortons were charming about it. Bettina said 'Forget it Sheila, but learn never to trust a journalist.' I sent a copy of my letter to the Gortons to the others who had been on board. They included Adrian Quist, Fred and Manya Kovaleski, Bruce and Pam Rose, their son Malcolm, Ainslie Gotto, Bo-Bo Faulkner, and a French couple whose names, after all these years, have escaped my memory—please forgive me. With the passage of time I suppose I should forgive David. We are good friends now, but for a long while were merely polite to each other!

---

From Mrs Gregory Blaxland (later Dame Helen Blaxland DBE)

*Seventy One Wallaroy Road*
*Woollahra*
*Sunday*

Dear Sheila
Welcome home—how was the world?

For the past year you must have been thinking me the most dilatory and evasive bitch, never having done anything about you and the Macquarie Club. There was a reason, which I have been working to overcome. The reason was a noisy and very spikey member of the Committee who was, for no known reason, violently anti-you. (To say 'no known reason' is absurd of course—she was patently jealous.)

Anyhow, one way and another she had so worked on the Committee that we were afraid that when your name came up we might be asked to withdraw it, a situation we did <u>not</u> enjoy contemplating as this would have been distasteful for you and anyhow, many of us would very much like to see you a member of the Club. I have spent a happy year quietly sabotaging cette type, and now all seems set fair.

This <u>long</u> preamble—forgive it—to explain why I am asking you if it is possible at such short notice to lunch at the Club next Wednesday, September 7.

The day is important as I am a great believer in showing a strong hand on these occasions—and Wednesday is the day that practically all the Committee stay to lunch after a meeting in the morning. I feel it would be a good idea for them to get the message.

I have collected Ann Challingsworth (as you know, present President), Florence, who will be happy to second you, Marie and Ruthie, who will also be very happy to be references, and Kate Stenning, who is, I understand, just going on to the Committee.

Margery Pagan and Joanie Bode will also be references but unfortunately can't come on Wednesday. Probably a very good thing actually, as <u>nine</u> women lunching together would be almost more than any of us could bare—excuse it—bear, even if for a very good reason.

So whatever you're doing on Wednesday, Sheila, <u>don't</u>. Please come to lunch with me instead.

As ever
Helen
in haste (which <u>may</u> explain this ill typed and ill
constructed letter).

Helen Blaxland was not only a highly esteemed 'personage' in
Sydney, but also a tactful, thoughtful friend. Of course I
accepted her invitation to lunch on that Wednesday with
those six mutual chums. Not long after, I was made a member
of the Macquarie Club. A few years later, there was a merger
(for want of a better word) with the Queen's Club in Elizabeth
Street, Sydney, our club closed and we automatically became
Queen's Club members. And I never did find out who was the
spiky, noisy member who opposed me ... I just hoped I would
never meet her in the ladies' 'loo or in a dark corridor!

---

From a florist in the St James's Street area
  *6 August 1976*

Dear Madam
With reference to your note dated 4th August, we have
tried to telephone you without success regarding the
Stephanotis plant.

In the first place, we do not know when this plant
was bought as it was not delivered by us, and must say
it has received very bad treatment to be in the
condition it is in at present.

Looking at the pot, it would appear this has been

left near to heat, probably a radiator as the plastic has become distorted.

In all the circumstances, we regret we cannot replace this.
Yours faithfully
JOAN PALMER LIMITED
(signed) J H C Palmer (Miss)

I was cross! The Stephanotis plant was given to me by my lover at the time for the anniversary of my deceased mother's birthday, so I wrote back:

Dear Miss Palmer
What a pity your letter makes you sound rather a disagreeable person (which I'm sure you are not), to whom the customer is always wrong.

I am sorry you question my word because firstly I told two members of your staff (including the manageress) the date the plant had been purchased and the sentimental reason for my not wanting it to die. Secondly my radiators have been turned off for months now, and although the pot was slightly distorted, that did not worry me.

How much nicer to have received the following letter ...

'I seem to have difficulty reaching you on the telephone so I write to say that our usual policy is not to replace plants that have been delivered by other people even though bought from us. But as you live so nearby, if you call in I would be happy to discuss

things with you and perhaps advise you the exact
treatment for Stephanotis plants.'

I am a member of the Consumers' Association
[similar in the UK to being a subscriber to *Choice* in
Australia] and I am sending a copy of this letter to
them, also to several friends who buy flowers from
your shop and the man who bought the Stephanotis
plant.

Yours faithfully

Sheila Scotter

---

From Dame Edith Bolte
*Mooloolaba*
*Queensland*
*11 June 1980*

Dear Miss Scotter

How very kind of you to send me such a lovely present.
It arrived on my birthday. I could not have had a nicer
present. We are at present in Queensland. We have a
tiny house up here and love coming up to the sunshine
away from the cold Victorian weather. Yesterday was
quite hot but today pleasantly warm.

I find your book most interesting. It is so well
named. I have not been well, the thought of eating was
not pleasant so I read about your beautiful food and
convince myself I have really enjoyed my meal.

So pleased to read you are a friend of Joan Ansett. I

agree she is a very super person. I very stupidly came away without your address, so if this is late in arriving you will know the reason.

Thank you ever so much for thinking of me in sending me your book. I am <u>thoroughly</u> enjoying reading it. I do hope I have the pleasure of meeting you again on our return to Victoria. With a very big thank you and my warmest good wishes
Jill Bolte

I had sent Dame Edith (known as Jill) a copy of my *Bedside Cookbook* after an evening spent with her and Sir Henry Bolte in Geelong. Sir Henry, then premier of Victoria, was to open an exhibition of sporting paintings in the Geelong Art Gallery. It was an early evening fundraising event and the organisers thought up the idea of making it a fun cocktail party. Invitations requested that ladies wear cocktail hats (much in vogue at the time). And I was asked to judge the prettiest and to present some prizes. Later we dined with the director of the gallery in what was then the best restaurant in Geelong, called The Source (now a popular wine bar and bistro and re-named Tousson). In those days The Source was frequented by gourmets from all over Victoria and one had to book well ahead to get a table. Both the Boltes were pretty heavy smokers, and I remember this evening mainly because Henry puffed away at a cigar throughout the entire meal, and Jill smoked more than a few cigarettes. It was agony for me but believe it or not I did not dare to complain … nor did anyone else!

From Richard Divall OBE
*Queen's College*
*University of Melbourne*
*11 October 1985*

Dear Sheila
I am writing a nice, personal but official letter, to thank
you <u>very deeply</u> and <u>warmly</u> for having arranged for
me to have your carpet. It means that the house at
Mansfield is going to be warm and I was saved a very
large amount of money—which I don't have at
present—by being able to have the house carpeted.

 Sheila, I'm really very grateful to you and I owe you
a very <u>big favour</u> at some stage. Never hesitate to ask
for it.
<u>With all my love</u>
Richard


That year I was re-decorating my home in South Yarra and
was very happy for my sand-beige carpets to have a good
home. I have never asked for that 'very big favour' because
during the intervening years I have been on the receiving end
of a few hurtful Divall remarks. Perhaps it is time they were
swept under that carpet ...

---

On 9 July 1996 I attended the Cointreau Ball in Sydney. My
escort was my American friend Dwane McHolick. This traditional ball means fancy dress is compulsory and I decided to

go as the Tsarina Alexandra II, wife of the Tsar Nicholas II. I asked Dwane whether he would come as Rasputin. He agreed. The next day he wrote to me, addressing it to my 'winter palace':

Your Imperial Majesty

It was indeed an high honour to escort Your Majesty to the Cointreau Ball last evening.

However I feel duty bound to caution Your Majesty about the dangers of accepting such invitations in future. As you will recall a number of attempts were made on our lives during the course of the evening (to say nothing of being transported like cattle in those run down army vehicles). You should speak to the Tsar about them, as well as the <u>raucous</u> behaviour of a number of his officers.

There was a first attempt to make us inebriated in that dismal parking lot and a second attempt in the barracks. (Don't your friends have a ballroom?) And of course we narrowly escaped being killed by the bombs after dinner (my ears are still ringing from the cacophony of the whole ordeal).

Luckily, we managed to flee before a worse fate befell us. Thank God I was wearing my cross which protected us and which gives such comfort to the Tsarevitch.

Being a Holy man, I could not help but notice a number of suspicious looking military types among the guests. (Who were all those people? Frankly a lot of them looked like gate crashers and you know the hoi polloi are always a danger.) If I may be so bold, Your Majesty, in the future it would be better to remain the Empress of Russia rather than the Daughter of the Regiment!

With prayers for your future safety, I remain
Your faithful and devoted servant
Rasputin

A sort of tongue-in-cheek letter which amused me, but Dwane was serious when he said 'I'll give you $500 not to ask me to come with you next year.' He didn't have to 'cough up'; the following year I wasn't invited.

# 7

A committee is too often a group that keeps minutes and loses hours.

**Anon.**

# Fundraising:
## Are Committees Really Necessary?

Back in 1986 *Harper's Bazaar* magazine (Australia) wrote:

Almost every day in Sydney and Melbourne, there is a ball, luncheon, cocktail party, theatre party or fashion show in the name of charity, and there are literally scores of charity committees to organise them. But the presidents of these committees are more than social butterflies flitting from function to fashion parade, pausing only to change their Versace daywear for a Ferre frock. They are a combination of public relations personnel, professional beggar, secretary and financier as well as having to appear as the perfect hostess.

It was their introduction to an article headed 'Sweet Charity' about four women, two from Sydney, two from Melbourne, who do a lot of fundraising. I was one. I am not sure that I actually fit their combined description, but having served on many committees and, in the latter part of my life, chaired quite a few, I entirely agree that chasing the ever-decreasing charity dollar is not for the so-called social butterflies of this world. It is darned hard work.

'Why do you still do it?' I have often been asked. My answer? I would love to have been born rich enough to be able to donate masses of money personally to charities. Instead, having no children and being able to do what I like when I like,

I have wanted to put something back. I really have had a pretty lucky sort of life, and have been fortunate enough to be able to contribute time and effort towards raising a few million dollars. But, I hasten to say, not entirely on my own. From this it can be seen that committees *are* (sometimes) necessary!

My sympathy has always been for the arts. I know that the blind, handicapped children, hospitals and so on are very worthy causes, but I also feel that artists are underpaid and overworked. As talented, creative dedicated contributors to the culture of this (or any) country, they are definitely undervalued.

My serious interest in opera started when I was living in London during the 1970s and George Harewood, who was general manager of the English National Opera, made me the honorary appeals director of the ENO Benevolent Fund. Later he asked me to do the same thing for their Corporate Membership Appeal, which (amazing as it may seem) asked for only £2500.

Our royal gala fundraising events were knock-out— hardly surprising when any musical concert or special opera performance was arranged by the Earl of Harewood and conducted by Charles (now Sir Charles) Mackerras, the artistic director of the ENO. We were able to raise large sums of money because almost any member of the royal family in those days helped sell seats at highly inflated prices—or, to be exact, their *name* on any invitation did. While Her Majesty Queen Elizabeth II was not exactly a fan of opera herself, her number one son and at the time the world's most eligible bachelor, the Prince of Wales, most certainly was. Prince Charles gave us great support and his patronage was invaluable. I met him on several occasions and liked him a lot (that was when he was single).

To sell a full house at The Coliseum (or Covent Garden) it is essential to form a large committee. Our chairman for each important fundraising event was Jenny Lee. Married to the socialist politician Aneuran Bevan, she had recently been made a baroness in her own right. She was also Minister for the Arts, the first ever (male *or* female) appointed in the UK, which may astound you. From this forthright, dynamic woman I learnt how to handle a large committee—which, of necessity, included some social butterflies (they sell seats) plus, inevitably, the odd person who, knowing they will never become a power, settles for becoming a nuisance. Jenny Lee always worked with a small executive group to decide pretty well all plans for the gala night well before the general meeting. She would then announce them and put them to the vote, *always* ending by saying 'I am sure that you are all going to approve of those exciting plans that have been decided by Lord Harewood and our executive committee. But if there is anyone who wishes to disagree, would they please stand up now, as (looking at her watch) I have to rush over to the House of Lords to vote against an important motion by Lord So-and-So.' It always seemed to work. Seldom did anyone stand up, and meetings were kept short.

Money raised from these really grand galas went to the English National Opera and Sadler's Wells Benevolent Fund, of which I was a trustee. Our main purpose was to help those now in retirement (or soon retiring)—people who had devoted their whole working lives to their profession, regardless of poor financial reward, and laid the foundation for the present

English National Opera. For many years we would need to support those who had given so much in return for so little and who may now rely solely on the State pensions (since they have been ineligible for company pension schemes). The fund was also needed for the present company. The ENO employed 500 people in a profession demanding the highest physical and mental standard. Inevitably financial help was needed in special cases of temporary misfortune. Whenever this occurred it was gratifying to know that the trustees were able to donate or lend money immediately.

In 1979 I was very happy to receive this letter from Lord Goodman, the Chairman of the ENO, sent on 20 September:

> Dear Miss Scotter
> I understand it is the unanimous wish of the Trustees
> of the Benevolent Fund that you would be reappointed
> for a further period of four years from the 22nd
> August last when your then current period expired.
> It is with great pleasure that I make this
> reappointment and would convey to you the grateful
> thanks of the Directors of the ENO for your most
> valuable help.
> Yours sincerely
> Goodman
> Chairman

Everyone has their own rules for successful fundraising. Here are some of mine, which seem to have worked for me and which I have often passed on to anyone new to charity work of this sort:

- Appoint to a committee only people who *contribute*, not those who just want their names on the writing paper and invitations.

- Before forming a new committee write down what is actually needed and then who can fill that need—for example, a lawyer, a printer or publisher or someone whose business will donate printing costs, at least one big corporate name who will be sympathetic to your cause, perhaps someone very rich (but only if generous!), an accountant for your treasurer, and so on ...

- I try not to inherit a committee, especially if it has been a large one. Better to form your own team and *keep it small*. For example, the Dame Joan Hammond Foundation which I chair is run by four of us: Peter Burch, deputy chairman; David Gibbs AM, honorary treasurer; and Noel Pelly AM, honorary secretary.

- Remember that, to get people to come back and support you another time, the fundraising event must *give good value* and be well organised ... therefore *planning well ahead is essential*. I will not take on anything at the last minute.

- To ensure good value always deal with caterers who understand that people paying, say, $100 or more expect good food. I always insist on tasting and seeing the presentation of dishes with the chef well beforehand.

- When raising money for charity *keep expenses low*—in other words, no four-colour or gilt edged invitations. I find writing a nice letter works well, unless of course someone *donates* invitations and then this should be given an acknowledgment.

- For a fundraising function to be totally successful, the

emphasis has to be on *enjoyment*. Over the years I must have asked literally thousands of people to host tables at grand balls, glittering gala dinners, and formal luncheons. My initial approach is usually verbal, sometimes a personal letter. Never have I been asked 'Who else is going to be there?' The people I know do not support gala charity dos merely to be seen; they go to enjoy themselves. Again most generous people I know are jolly busy. They receive umpteen invitations (not only mine)—so, unless they feel they and their friends are going to really enjoy an evening, one can hardly blame them if they decide not to accept but perhaps send a nice donation.

Occasionally the sensible rule of planning well ahead when fundraising has been broken, with no ill-effect.

It was the end of 1974 and I was living in London. Almost within hours of the devastation caused by Cyclone Tracy in Darwin a couple of days before Christmas, the Australian High Commissioner in London, John Armstrong, contacted me wanting me to join a committee to arrange for a fundraising event to help the people of Darwin. John had arranged for the switchboard at Australia House to be open all through Christmas and, among enquiries from families and relations, he had calls from many entertainers in Britain who knew and loved this country and wanted to help in any way.

A gala variety show was planned for 9 February 1975, a Sunday night, in the Prince of Wales Theatre on Leicester Square. Sir Bernard Delfont donated the theatre and allowed the glamorous sets being used by Danny La Rue in his current performance to be used for this concert. The committee, chaired by Ruth Nye, consisted of Dick Bentley, Geoffrey Chard, John McCallum CBE, Anona Winn MBE, Elizabeth Murphy and myself.

My main job was to be the contact with the Palace for a royal Guest of Honour and to organise as many VIP Australians as possible to pay for the expensive seats. Here I had valuable help from Squadron Leader David Checketts in Buckingham Palace who, at short notice, got us HRH the Princess Anne (then Mrs Mark Phillips), as well as Bruce Gyngell who was then head of ITV in the UK. Whilst all the stars and other artists were donating their services, we had to pay the musicians in the orchestra. Bruce called Kerry Packer to see whether he would underwrite this cost for us. He not only did this, but he arranged for the whole show to be tele-recorded for transmission in Australia by the Nine Network, with revenue from advertising going to the Darwin Fund. Princess Anne was in one of her good moods and in spite of the fact that Mark Phillips had to leave very early the next morning to join his regiment in Germany, she stayed much later than scheduled to meet all the generous performers. They included some pretty top names in show business: Anna Neagle, Derek Nimmo, Maggie Fitzgibbon, Rod Hull, Emu, June Bronhill, Jimmy Tarbuck, Danny La Rue and his dancers and singers, Doreen Wells and Patrice Bart (from the Paris Opera Ballet) and Frank Ifield. These big-hearted artists were introduced by other big stars: Honor Blackman, Miriam Karlin, Moira Lister, Googie Withers and Emlyn Williams, each addressing the audience with a few words of their own.

The whole show was staged and directed by Freddie Carpenter with music by the Prince of Wales Orchestra and the Herald Trumpeters of Her Majesty's Royal Marines.

All in all it was what I might be forgiven for calling a right royal night. We raised over £22,000 and our small committee managed to organise it *within six weeks*! I still have my souvenir programme, signed by most of the famous. I sent one to David Checketts and told him the amount we had raised. A letter arrived for me from Buckingham Palace:

Dear Sheila
Many thanks for your letter of the 19th February and for the copy of the Royal Gala Variety Show for Darwin. I am delighted it was such a success both from the point of view of an evening's entertainment and from fundraising. The next one ought to be in Darwin! Yours ever David.

I should add to my personal rules for successful fundraising the importance of writing thank-you letters—to donors of prizes, sponsors of special events, in fact anyone who has been particularly helpful, and that can include hotel staff, caterers, decorators and so on. I try to write most of my letters by hand, so I endeavour to compose one that can be sent to everyone concerned, get them photocopied perfectly and hand-address the envelopes in the same black ink.

When it comes to collecting money from those who have pledged it, I have found that people respond almost immediately to a handwritten note. This was certainly the case in London in September 1979 when money was needed to launch the Sir Robert Menzies Memorial Trust. (This Trust's objectives are to create scholarships in law and sports medicine for Australians at Oxford, Cambridge, Edinburgh and St Andrews Universities, to establish a centre for Australian studies in London, and to sponsor British postgraduate students in Australia. It was launched on 12 June 1979.) The chairman was Lord Carrington KCMG MC, and the appeal director was a good chum of mine, Captain Stephen Stuart CBE RN, who inveigled me into joining his committee. On Sunday 23 September 1979, we took over the whole of Hyde Park and held a mass of different fundraising activities involving public participation. Some were pre-planned and I was mainly involved that day with organising the Menzies Day Sponsored Run and obtaining sponsors for certain celebrities to do a lap (or more) round the Serpentine in Hyde Park. One lap was two miles.

Most of the celebrities were youngish athletes, but our High Commissioner, Sir Gordon Freeth, gallantly agreed to take up the challenge—providing I would get him sponsors. Through personal friends and pro-Aussies living or visiting in the UK we got a pretty good collection. The names included Robert Carrier, Frederick Fox, Lady McKay, Lady Melchett, Lord Harewood, Mark and Diana Mackenzie-Charrington (parents of Sophie, the young letter writer), Morris West, Admiral Sir Anthony Griffin, Commander and Mrs Hugh Eaton, Freddie Carpenter, William Haffenden, Jean Pratten, Hans Rueb and even the editor of *Jogging* magazine.

My handwritten letter of thanks read as follows:

At my request you very kindly agreed to sponsor HE

The Australian High Commissioner for £5 per lap of the Serpentine. Our robust 65-year-young Sir Gordon Freeth ran <u>2 laps</u> (4 miles!) which means that, with generous sponsorship such as yours, he personally raised over £600 for the Sir Robert Menzies Memorial Trust.

I enclose an addressed envelope for your cheque of £10 and send you my very warm thanks for helping in this way.

Sheila Scotter

Not one of my best letters but everyone's cheque came in within the week ... Enclosing an addressed envelope probably helped!

Speaking of letters, I have found that it is sometimes wise to 'warn' people *well before* the date of certain events. These letters I send personally. One event that was a complete sell-out with a long waiting list was when Mr Willi Martin of Sydney's Park Hyatt Hotel offered to donate a dinner from which the entire proceeds could go to one of my favourite charities. I chose the Australian Ballet.

This particular gala dinner was organised by my preferred type of committee—only three people: Noel Pelly, his assistant Amanda Lamb and myself. I wrote by hand 'Please keep 2 December free' and gave a brief outline of the evening, explaining that seating was limited and concluding with:

This particular dinner will be more like a private party of friends and it would most certainly be enhanced by your presence. So, if this exciting night appeals to you,

**Above left:** My favourite, to-wear-forever Balenciaga evening raincoat. Bought in a sale in New York (reduced from $400 to only $60) about twenty-five years ago and still going to theatre, opera and ballet black-tie first nights. **Above right:** The red dress designed by John Cavill and worn only once, on 2 December 1990, (see pages 7 and 125) at the Windsor Hotel, Melbourne. (Photo courtesy of *New Idea*) **Below left:** At Ettalong beach with the only member of my family who lives in Australia, my cousin Barrie Peters. (Photo Ethna Peters) **Below right:** Christmas 1996 at Woomargama Homestead in New South Wales, with my hostess and long-time friend Margaret Darling. (Photo Jacinta Mirams)

**Above left:** At the July 1996 Cointreau Ball in Sydney. Yours truly as the Tsarina Alexandra II (yes it is I) and my escort Dwane McHolick as my protector Rasputin. (Photo Josh Ellis)
**Above right:** Judging the fashion at the 1996 Melbourne Cup Breakfast at the Pavilion Restaurant in St Kilda (since renamed Donovans) with Lady Celestria Noel, the social editor of *Harper's & Queen* magazine in the UK. (Photo Rennie Ellis) **Below left:** Peter Burch, deputy chairman of the Dame Joan Hammond Foundation, with the chairman. A portrait of Dame Joan in the background. (Photo courtesy *Herald Sun*) **Below right:** After lunch at the Berkeley Hotel in London with Joseph and Estée Lauder, October 1977.

**Above:** Nearing Noumea on the maiden voyage of the luxury sailing cruise ship *Club Med II*, which departed Sydney on 11 December 1992. John Truscott, Rea Francis and self. (Photo courtesy of Club Med) **Below left:** With Dame Pattie Menzies as guests of Westpac during the America's Cup trials on Port Phillip Bay. **Below right:** Bernard Goodman and his adorable old English sheep dog Cashmere in Bernard's swiming pool at Quogue on Long Island.

**Above left:** With Princess Yasmin Khan (daughter of Rita Hayworth) in her apartment on Central Park West, New York. Photographed by Ted Lustig who was bringing her out to Melbourne to raise funds for Alzheimer's research. **Above right:** Dulcie Boling and I at the Victorian Arts Centre. (Photo Rennie Ellis) **Below left:** At Donovans restaurant in St Kilda when Lady Renouf and I were invited to meet Christian Feron of the Crillon Hotel, Paris, on 10 December 1997. (Photo Bob Hart) **Below right:** With Madame Isabelle Costa de Beauregard (then French Consul General) at the Melbourne Town Hall to celebrate the 14th of July 1997.

**Above left:** With Sarah Myer at the 70th birthday of Bails Myer in the garden at 'Cranlana'. **Above right:** At the wedding reception of Margaret Darling's daughter, Clare Darling, and Andrew Cannon at Woomargama Homestead, New South Wales, with Florence Anderson, Clare's grandmother. **Below left:** Portrait of my cousin General Sir William Scotter, painted for the City of Carlisle when he was given the Freedom of the City. **Below right:** At the opening night in Canberra of 'Boswell for the Defence' with (left to right) Bill Haffenden, Lady Murray, Sir Brian Murray and co-producer Bill May.

**Opposite top:** The table 'MELBOURNE SALUTES SYDNEY' at the opening of the Park Lane Hotel (now Sheraton on the Park). Left to right: Noel Pelly, Beverley Sutherland Smith, Kath Clarke, John MacKinnon, Douglas Butler, Peter Rowland, SS, Rupert Clarke, Susie Rowland and John Truscott. **Opposite centre:** The day I received my AM, photographed by Bill Wilson with John Truscott, Bill Haffenden and Sonia MacMahon (1992). **Opposite bottom left:** With long-time friend Freddie Fox (the Monarch's milliner) at a gathering of the Millinery Association of Victoria on 7 November 1997. (Photo Bruce Kirby) **Opposite bottom right:** On my 75th birthday with Bill Wilson in the Peter Rowland Gallery restaurant.

**Above left:** Ruth Woolard, my 'adopted' New York American sister, and I, photographed by her husband Paul in their penthouse apartment in Manhattan. **Above right:** My other 'adopted' American sister, Alberta Liljestrand, lives in Hawaii. Here, we are cooking together in her kitchen during my visit in 1997, photographed by husband Howard. **Below left:** With Cardinal O'Connor of New York, who is flanked by an Anglican (me) and my Jewish beau Bernard Goodman at a fundraising gala dinner in 1988. **Below right:** A celebration hug with John Truscott after the opening night of his successful second Melbourne International Festival, 1989.

These legs were meant for walking and in February 1994 they were on the runway in Sydney's Museum of Modern Art. At 73 years old I modelled for Trent Nathan when he launched his new smart-sport-casual line for Myer—Grace Bros. (The photo was taken for Lawrence Money who ran it in his 'Spy' column in the *Sunday Age*.)

will you pencil the date in your diary <u>now</u> ... and I
shall of course follow up with a formal invitation
together with all relevant details later on.
Very warmly
Sheila S

I found out later on that this fundraising evening yielded for
the Australian Ballet a great deal more money—thirty per
cent more—than a gala ball held a few months previously and
run by a committee of over twenty, who attended several
longish meetings. We had two working lunches with sandwiches in Noel Pelly's office ... but we did have efficient
Amanda to cope with the mailing of invitations *and* our letters of thanks.

Sometimes one can fundraise in reverse. By that I mean
help the arts not by *raising* money for them but by *saving*
them having to spend it on certain extras, such as hospitality,
which they would dearly like to extend but which tight budgets do not allow.

For example, Leo Schofield, when artistic director of the
Melbourne Festival, was always anxious that leading international artists were not just left to return to their hotel rooms
when not performing. In 1996 he asked whether I would help
by approaching several restaurants to see whether they would
donate a dinner, lunch or brunch for, say, two, four or six (or
whatever suited). As hostess I was then to invite interesting
Victorians for the visitors to meet. The plan worked well and
the only charge to the festival budget was the odd taxi fare.

One who visited in 1996 was Miss Irene Worth CBE
whom Leo asked me 'to especially "duchess"'. 'I think you

will both get on,' he said. Happily we did. I just adored her. This brilliant, legendary actress, who was in her eighties, had much more energy than yours truly, and I am not exactly lacking in that department. We covered a lot of ground as she was curious to see and do so much. I made a report (really rough notes) for the festival management of the days and nights between her arrival on 10 October and 1 November when she left for the Northern Territory and Kakadu—on her own. The report was rather long as it included 'duchessing' Irene Worth for about three weeks! Fortunately I had help and generosity from many friends, including Marjory Lynch, who gave Irene lunch and a guided tour of the National Gallery of Victoria; and Christina Stitt, who drove her all round Melbourne and took her shopping at the Victoria Market. Both Marjory and Christina were amazed at this octogenarian's energy. So was Loretta Wilson when she 'lunched' her at The Pavilion (since renamed Donovans) and took her to visit Melbourne's famous zoo. When Irene left the country a letter arrived from Leo, saying:

> Dearest Sheila
> What a smashing job you did looking after Irene. Peter
> Eyre had warned me (in the most affectionate way)
> that she would be 'high maintenance', and I knew of
> no one who could take care of her the way you would.
> I've now seen the list of outings you organised for our
> guest. Phew! Only someone with your stamina could
> have stood the pace. I do hope that, when I hit eighty,
> my mind is as enquiring and my energy running at the
> same level as Ms Worth's.

But it is only one of the many, many ways in which you showed your remarkable generosity and flair during my time in Melbourne. I had the feeling that, as the Americans say, you were always there for me and I am eternally grateful that you were.

I have been feeling quite dejected leaving so many good chums behind. Despite almost non-stop sunshine here, I am missing Melbourne and the only things mitigating my blue mood are proximity to my family and Sydney friends and my garden which is looking terrific. Do please come and see it next time you are in Sydney.

Thanks, dear Sheila, for your unswerving support across three Festivals.

With great love and affection

Leo

---

I have always maintained that, in the arts scene, there are far too many people who stay on Boards long past their use-by date, and that some Boards are overloaded. I remember the Victoria State Opera (a part-time opera company) having at one time, eighteen Board members.

On 5 June 1983 I wrote to Sir Rupert Hamer, chairman of the VSO, saying:

I know that you have been aware of my often expressed personal belief that 3 years is the maximum time to serve on cultural councils or Boards administering large sums of public money. As I shall not be at tomorrow's Board Meeting, may I ask you to do something for me? Will you kindly, on my behalf, thank those colleagues who not only gave me support as Honorary Appeals Director, but also practical assistance and generous contributions to many fundraising events which helped me raise quite large sums of money for the VSO during my 3 years. I shall of course be pleased to continue raising dollars for the Company through the Foundation ... assuming this will be needed and appreciated.

Copies were sent to Lord Harewood, Sir Charles Mackerras, Mr Paul Clarkson, and all trustees of the VSO Foundation.

Although much relieved to be off that particular Board, I was quite happy to continue my involvement with the VSO Foundation, which was established in 1981 to strengthen the financial base for the opera company. I was made vice-chairman and responsible for the raising of funds (in those days this was quite something, as to get big dollars from the corporate sector, a Melbourne Old Boys' Network-type chairman seemed to be de rigueur!). Money was raised in various ways: a fabulous masked ball at the Hilton on the Park, a grand gala performance starring Kiri Te Kanawa in the Melbourne Concert Hall, the first 'Opulent Event' in the newly 'revived' Myer Mural Hall, an 'Absolute Ball' to celebrate the tenth anniversary season of the VSO and in August 1982 a 'Salute to the new Melbourne Concert Hall', to name a few. The nitty-gritty work was carried out mainly by a small efficient group of volunteers: Douglas Butler, Marilyn

Davis (currently Darling) and myself, with paid assistance from Penny Willington, Avril Everingham and Nicholas Heyward of the VSO.

The remarkable increase in foundation membership was due to our monthly lunches at which guest speakers over the years included Dr Jean Battersby AO, John Hopkins OBE, Brian White, Anna Russell, Jenifer Eddy, Phillip Henry, Anne Woolliams, Dr John Marum, John Truscott AO, Professor Claudio Veliz, Hon. Charles Race Mathews MLA, Leo Schofield, Dame Margaret Guilfoyle DBE, Dennis Pryor, Lady Tait, Paul Clarkson, Dame Joan Hammond DBE CMG, Professor Geoffrey Blainey AO, Noel Mangin, Lady Murray CStJ, Donald McDonald AO, Irvin Rockman CBE, Elke Neidhart, Noel Pelly AM, Sir Claus Moser, John Cargher AM, Annette Allison, Martin Carlson, Richard Divall OBE, Ross Campbell, Suzie Howie, Roland Rocchiccioli, Dr Ron Quirk, Sue Nattrass, Dr Rodney Wilson, Michael Gray, George Fairfax AM and Geoffrey Chard OBE ... hoping my memory has not left out too many, and reminding you that this is all pre-1990.

While an individual lunch did not raise as many dollars as a gala dinner, ball, or concert, collectively these popular monthly get-togethers were definitely responsible for cultivating long-term supporters for the Victoria State Opera company.

While enjoying my involvement with the foundation and its success financially, I eventually became concerned with the way money donated by the public was being used. I was also critical of the way the Board was constructed, and expressed my misgivings in private talks with some of the directors. Two of them agreed with my opinion of the general management

... but, sad to say, nothing was done. I left the foundation in December 1989, proud of my contribution and pleased I was to be recognised in the VSO programmes as 'Founding Trustee'.

In May 1997 the Victoria State Opera was voluntarily wound up. When this finally happened I felt desperately sad for the many people who had donated big money themselves, and for those who had generously helped me to raise a great many dollars over the years. John Truscott had been right. Whenever we discussed policies and problems that concerned the VSO, he always made the comment: 'The way they are going, one day they will go under.' If John had been alive in May 1997 I think he, too, would have felt very sad.

In a small way I have helped to raise money for the National Gallery of Victoria and thoroughly enjoyed doing so ... particularly on one occasion that involved no work at all! I donated a pair of unusual French boots to Robyn Healy, the highly respected curator of fashion and textiles. I had bought them from Courrèges when I was living in Paris. Designed by François Villon, they were in excellent condition, not having been worn since the 1960s, and Healy included them in the important 1996 exhibition 'Couture to Chaos'. They were photographed for postcards to be sold in the gallery shop's large collection of postcards and greeting cards. They cost only eighty cents each, and there is no prize for guessing who bought them by the dozen. I use them still for amusing thank you notes and have to confess it is because my gift is credited on the back and I have never had my name in print on a postcard before.

Another time, with invaluable help from my friends

John Truscott and Gordon Ryan, I organised a glamorous gala dinner in the Peter Rowland Gallery restaurant on 8 September 1992 ... no speeches, just scrumptious food and wines after a private preview of the stunning Balenciaga exhibition that Healy had organised in conjunction with Madame Marie Andrée Jouve, Chef des Archives of Balenciaga in Paris. Our guest of honour was His Excellency Monsieur Philippe Baude, the French Ambassador. The money raised was the first step towards a fashion council to support the NGV's Fashion and Textile department. It is very satisfying to know how fundraising money is spent and I was thrilled to read in a letter from Robyn Healy the following May (1993) that they had been able to purchase a 1956 Christian Dior evening dress, also an Emilio Pucci jump suit (1969) for the gallery's fashion collection, as well as being able to afford a costly restoration of a Balenciaga 'infanta' dress that had recently been donated.

One particular fundraising committee on which I am honoured to serve, and on which I have a lot of fun, has nothing to do with the arts. On my return to Melbourne in 1980, I was asked by my friend John MacKinnon, who knew of my great love of cricket, to join The Lord's Taverners as a founding member. I accepted immediately. He then asked whether I would help with—yes, you've guessed it—fundraising.

For those unfamiliar with The Lord's Taverners, our aims and objectives are to encourage and promote the playing of cricket, especially amongst underprivileged and disadvantaged children. We raise money to provide cricket facilities, including grounds, practice areas, competitions and equipment. My contribution is to help organise most of their fundraising functions. I am not an authority on the game but, as you will have gathered by now, am crazy about it.

The main money-raising event is the Taverners' traditional Boxing Day breakfast at the Hilton on the Park. Other funds are raised from lunches or dinners with guest speakers, and our annual Trivial Pursuit nights. Invitations for the latter, incidentally, list witty Craig Willis, committee member, as Master of Ceremonies and Question Master together with myself as 'barrel girl'—some girl at well over three score years and ten! ... and a rather bossy barrel lady at that, which I am told is all part of the fun. However, in July 1996 when I was unable to attend, naughty Craig announced 'Ladies and gentlemen. I have good news. This is a totally Sheila-free evening.' I later heard that everyone clapped. So the next year I asked for a round of applause for being present. I got it. But when I sat down Craig announced, 'Yes, the Headmistress is back, folks.'

In 1993, to my amazement, I was asked by the editor of *The Cricketer* magazine to write a page for their Celebrity Spot for the April issue. As I was on the Victorian Committee of the Lord's Taverners I decided to agree to do my best, thinking that it might further our cause. The title of my piece was 'Cricket Nuts & Loving It'. And I wrote that I would like to have a dollar for each time I have been asked by women friends 'How can you possibly love watching cricket?' My confession that, for a few years I even enjoyed playing the game is generally received with even greater disbelief.

At St Swithun's School, Winchester (UK), where I was educated, our games mistress was vice-captain of England, a renowned wicket keeper with the comic name of Betty Snowball. This pocket sized dynamo turned me into a pretty nifty slip-fielder as well as a reasonable bat. Because I was no good at bowling, I hated doing it; but Miss Snowball made everyone have a go—which in my case was always humiliating.

My love of cricket may be inherited. The whole Scotter family comprised what I call cricket nuts and I have enjoyed watching village and county matches since the age of ten. My father was a member of the Hampshire County Cricket Club. As a family we seldom missed an 'at home' game in Southampton, Bournemouth or Portsmouth. Our favourite ground was Bournemouth Dean Park where we brought delicious picnic lunches and lounged all day in deck chairs in front of the (then) tiny pavilion.

In those days Hampshire was consistently at the bottom of the ladder. However, one day at Southampton we had a moment of glory when we bowled the mighty Australians out for 117! Bradman was not playing and Keith Miller made the top score of 39 (which, if my memory is correct, included three consecutive sixes). This was back in 1948. I retained my membership of the HCC but switched my loyalty from Hampshire when I came to live in Australia.

I recall one Test in Manchester (which I followed on the radio during the night) when the Aussies were having a dreadful time. England had knocked up a huge score during the first two days. From Sydney I cabled a Lancashire beau of mine (Derek Roberts, another cricket nut): 'How about three days of good old Manchester rain?' Well, believe it or not, the tear ducts of the heavens actually let go and it was still raining when his reply came: 'Your telegram arrived in thunderstorm. Postman struck by lightning. Lay off the witchcraft: signed Mancunian.'

Yes, my support is always for the Aussies, even when sitting with Pommy chums at Lord's in London ... more so when among the kind that call people by their surnames. I shall never forget, during the 1970s when I was living in London, how I arrived just before the lunch interval to find our No. 4 at the crease. 'Gosh, don't tell me Greg is out,' I said to myself, but aloud. 'My dear woman,' came a response from one patronising chap. 'He is captain of England and we are fielding.' 'Listen chum, *my* Greg is a Chappell,' I said. '*Your* Greig is Tony to me.' End of conversation.

Because I had such a privileged childhood, with cricket-loving parents, I am honoured and proud to be on the Victorian Committee of the Taverners. Our president is Dr John Lill, the chairman Quentin Miller, and patron and twelfth man HRH the Duke of Edinburgh. Not unexpectedly, the committee consists almost entirely of males ... all truly delightful gentlemen who, every time I offer to resign and be replaced by someone younger, tell me 'Sheila, we don't want you for your body.' So, to make a ghastly pun, I am *not out* yet! Amongst the aforementioned truly delightful gents I am bound to be considered a bit of a philistine as I definitely prefer to watch the 'one day' matches, not being able to spare the four or five days to *attend* a Test match. But thank goodness for television and radio.

# 8

Plan for this world as if you expect to live forever: But plan for the hereafter as if you expect to die tomorrow.

**Ibn Garibol**

# Loved Ones Departed
## (or Why I Envy the Angels)

So many people speak of others who have died as having 'departed' or 'passed away' or being 'no longer with us'. For me certain people are not dead, but thought of constantly and talked about as if they were still with us. I feel sorry for anyone who does not believe in God and the hereafter. I do. However, at my age I realise I shall have to pay more attention to the latter part of the saying 'Plan for this world as if you are going to live forever, but plan for the hereafter as if you expect to die tomorrow.' With my past, I think that the Almighty will expect a little overtime when it comes to saying my prayers.

If I am alive when this book is published, I shall still be praying that the Almighty will admit me to heaven ... if not, I hope St Peter has let me in! I want to meet up with my darling parents, my two brothers and many beloved friends. The first person whom I would like to greet and have hug me is John Truscott. I miss this man more than anyone I have known during my long life and not a day passes without my thinking of him. Ours was an extraordinary friendship, a precious relationship ... alas for only thirteen years.

We met in Melbourne in 1980. He died on Sunday 5 September 1993. He was only fifty-seven. While John's death was absolutely devastating for me, it was a shocking loss for all Australia. As Sue Nattrass (a close friend, then general manager of the Victorian Arts Centre, now artistic director of the Melbourne International Festival) said in her eulogy at his funeral: 'John Truscott touched the hearts of many people, as a friend, as a colleague, as a lover and loved one, or simply as one we have admired from afar.' It may sound bizarre to you, but I sometimes re-read the eloquent words of another close friend, distinguished artist and theatre director Nigel Triffitt: 'There are great men who make others feel small and great men who make all around them feel important. John Truscott was the latter—an inspiration, a role model and a hero to me.' Headed 'A guiding light who pursued excellence', Nigel's moving obituary for the *Australian* newspaper (6 September 1993) is at my bedside … it is hard to keep back tears whenever I read it.

Like me, Sue and Nigel both knew the private John. Everyone knew of his passion for work, but I found him unexpectedly shy, almost annoyingly humble when one was aware of his genius … caring, kind, fiercely generous and passionately loyal, a champion of those he loved.

John used to call me on the telephone almost every morning at 8.15, and often again later in the day. While he was working sixteen hours a day designing the interior of the Victorian Arts Centre he definitely needed tender loving care. Many an evening, he would call in on his way home and discuss problems of the day with me over a simple home-cooked meal. For nearly two years we were next-door neighbours: John had rented the house of my close friends Gordon and Marieta Robinson while they were overseas in Venezuela and Spain. While I enjoyed cooking for Truscott, he was not an easy man to persuade to eat properly. That sounds like a British nanny talking!—I mean proper healthy foods. No matter how hard I tried to get him to eat fresh green salads with his meal, he'd say, 'You eat it, I prefer another cigarette.' (He was one of the *very* few men I would tolerate smoking at the table. I hated *it*, but loved *him*, so there was always a lidded silver ashtray placed by his table napkin.)

John adored soup, especially the one I often made with mushrooms. I used to produce this in a jiffy just by sautéing some chopped onion in butter until soft and adding a whole lot of mushrooms. These I would wipe clean (not wash) and put (stalks and all) in the blender, then add to the onions. I would sprinkle with a dash of flour, stir well in and cover with chicken stock. Finally I would bring the lot to the boil and simmer for about ten to fifteen minutes. After seasoning to taste I would serve this to John with a dollop of cream in the soup plate. I felt flattered when, in a thank-you letter for my support over the three years of John's tenure with the Melbourne International Festival, of which he was artistic director, he said at the end, 'I feel fortunate indeed to have you as a friend and as the best soup maker I know.'

While I was not involved officially with anything to do with the Arts Centre, unofficially I did help by networking privately to raise funds and patronage for a few projects that John was passionate to include, about which the accountants were saying 'We can't do this, there is not enough money.' John's reply was always the same: 'Oh yes, we can. We'll get the f ... money.' And he usually did.

For nearly a year during 1987/88 I actually worked *for* him, and was highly paid to do so. Truscott was based in

Brisbane while designing the site for World Expo '88 and employed by Thiess Watkins (Construction) Limited, the project managers. At John's request they appointed me a consultant to their Creative Division. My role was to liaise with Truscott to obtain money plus certain material contributions for this great bicentennial exhibition. I was up and down to and from Brisbane but based in Melbourne, as most head offices where decisions involving considerable financial support were made were in the southern states, especially Victoria. For example, John needed tons of BHP steel, sheets of Pilkington bullet-proof glass, the loan for six months of the fine Minton porcelain Loch Aird peacock from Warrnambool ... to name a few items, not to mention the big dollars from big banks.

Sometimes I wondered whether we'd be successful, but we were. And I say 'we' because John made my job easier by telling me that, *whenever* I was having a tough time in negotiations, he was always available on the end of a telephone to explain any technical details or answer complicated questions, *no matter what he was doing*. There was no wretched answering machine or 'I'll call you back' nonsense with this genius. No wonder people adored working with him.

However, like any genius, he would be difficult at times, but only if he had indulged in too much Scotch and was overtired. To quote Nigel Triffitt:

He was a consummate professional and used every weapon at his command to achieve his goal. Charming, witty and intense, he could move from volcanic rage to motherly love in an instant, switch his public persona to the private one in a way that made me feel privileged to be there.

I wish I'd been privileged to have known him longer than thirteen years ... When I die I have arranged to be buried next to John's grave in the Nangana Emerald–Macclesfield Cemetery at Avonsleigh in Victoria's glorious Dandenong Ranges.

---

I was living in London when my parents died, within only a few weeks of each other. My father was nearly ninety and Mummy was eighty-six and a half. Neither was ill; they both just died. My brother Guy and I, of course, observed their wishes to be cremated after a funeral service in our local church, very close to Oak Tree Cottage, Ringwood, Hampshire, where they lived. The nearest crematorium was in Bournemouth, which meant no gravestones for them in the little church on Poulner Hill which we had attended as a family.

Guy and I wondered what we could do to preserve their memory. We did not particularly want a brass plaque, nor would my parents want it. However, as the church was short of quality prayer books, and so many parishioners did not always bring their own, with the padre's permission we decided to donate the quantity required—from memory about eighty (it was only a small congregation.) Inside each prayer book we had printed:

This prayer book is in memory of Harold and Winifred Scotter who lived on Poulner Hill and worshipped at this church 1937–1977.
Given by Sheila and Guy Scotter, their daughter and son.

Sudden death is always a shock, no matter at what age, but Guy and I both thanked the good Lord for the fact that neither of our parents suffered pain or endured any lingering illness. I recall that we said at the time, knowing our parents were ardent cricket followers, that Daddy would probably have said, 'Well, we both had a good innings.' I am hoping I have inherited their genes.

Alas, sadly, my beloved brother did not. He died only ten years later (in January 1987) and he, poor darling, did suffer a rather long illness—stoically, like the good soldier he was. I was in Melbourne and had been warned by my ex-sister-in-law Carol Stratton, who had just been on the telephone to Lymington Hospital and learnt that Guy was about to lose consciousness and was near the end. I immediately called the sister in charge who said, while I could not speak to him, to hold on, she would take a message and come back to me. The message was 'all my love and he would be happy to know that the Brits were starting to beat the hell out of the Aussies in the Test match which had just begun' (they eventually won it by an innings and fourteen runs). Sister came back to say he had definitely registered my message and he had a happy smile. He died an hour and twenty minutes later.

I did not fly over to England for his funeral. I knew that Guy would agree with me that a much more sensible idea would be to spend the money on 'shouting' a holiday for Penny, my sister-in-law, who had been such a devoted and caring wife during some pretty trying years. I arranged this in February 1988 and, with the help of my friends, she had a well-deserved fun holiday.

My youngest brother Richard Scotter drowned in 1940

during the war. He was only a child and still at prep school. I was at the Royal College of Aeronautical Engineering at the time. I should explain.

During World War II most of my girlfriends joined up in the women's branches of either the Army, Navy or Air Force. Although I come from an army family I could not see myself doing this. (As I have said, I do not respect rank.) The *Times* newspaper published an advertisment for a limited number of women students to study at the Royal College of Aeronautical Engineering—from memory, twenty-five each year. As we were just about surviving the Battle of Britain, and London and major cities were being bombed beyond recognition, the situation looked grim. 'Oh,' I thought, 'I'll see if I can get an interview.' I did, and amazingly was accepted to this short course of eighteen months. No degree or anything to boast of—just a little knowledge about a lot ... mainly metallic materials. I was then offered a job (well, *allocated* one, as this was a government-sponsored scheme) in the Ministry of Aircraft Production. It sounds grand. In fact it was in the inspection division, checking on records of tensile strength in metal components being made in factories all over the London area. I enjoyed myself but never thought of making a career in this field, despite the compliment of being offered a job with a firm called High Duty Alloys when the war ended.

I shall never forget the day, just a few weeks into my aeronautical engineering course, when I was told that the principal wanted to see me in his office immediately. Wondering whether I had done something wrong, I heard the dreadful news about Richard and was also told that my father was on his way to collect me and that we would drive to join Mummy in the New Forest.

Richard's sudden death shocked us all. Privately, for me, the most shattering part was witnessing the grief of my parents. I had never seen my father cry before and have never forgotten the effect this had on me. For months I refused to go to church, finding it jolly hard to understand how God could allow this tragedy to happen to someone so young. As they say, He moves in mysterious ways.

---

I gave the following eulogy at the Memorial Service of Thanksgiving for the life of Patsy Fox, St Joseph's Church, Edgecliff, Sydney, 28 May 1993:

When Frank Fox first asked me to speak this morning, I pleaded not to, having never given a eulogy for anyone before. But then I could almost hear our darling Patsy saying, 'Oh come on, She-She, you can do this for me and for Frank and Lisa [their daughter] ... Just don't go on too long. Don't exaggerate and don't be too long.'

Well it would be hard for *anyone* not to say flattering things about Patsy Fox. I have known her for about thirty-eight years ... back in the days when we lived near each other in the Potts Point/Kings Cross area of Sydney. She was then a very young widow, Patsy Minton, and being wooed very seriously by young Frank Fox whom we all know eventually married her.

I recall that I thought she was the most feminine, fastidious woman I knew. I have never changed my opinion. Perhaps English–Scottish parents were responsible for her flawless skin, that neat figure, even her bouncy sexy walk (nearly always in high heels). Patsy never seemed to alter: always immaculately groomed and I don't think anyone remembers seeing her without her make-up. In fact she had confided to one close friend here in the church today, 'I don't even let Frank see me without my eyebrows on.'

This ultra-feminine woman (who incidentally was never known to wear pants, trousers or jeans) had an uncanny way of *pretending* to be bossy. At the entrance of their townhouse in Edgecliff there was a notice that said 'The opinions expressed by the husband in this house are not necessarily those of the management.'

Patsy Fox was one of the world's givers—never a taker. She was teasingly called by her own family 'The Minister for Other People's Affairs'. Her concern for friends, even acquaintances was constant, totally genuine and rather maternal—very maternal actually—she was always cooking special dishes for, dropping in on or shopping for elderly neighbours, or taking a basket of goodies to young people whom she thought were not eating (what she called) proper food.

We shared a godson, Tony Potts, who is here in church today. He was responsible for her nickname ... also for mine as it happens. For when he was only at the Dad-dad-Mum-mum limited vocabulary stage, his name for Patsy was 'Party' and he called me 'She-She'. Both names stuck and are still used by family and close mutual friends. You could say that Party was well named. She excelled as a hostess and many of us here today have enjoyed generous Fox hospitality.

Some of my own nicest memories are of days spent on board their magnificent motor cruiser 'Sea Vixen'. Here Frank got his own back in the notice department. On board he had framed the definition of a vixen: 'A female fox, a quarrelsome woman, wayward, perverse and not easily managed', adding 'Any resemblance these definitions may have to the qualities of the wife and daughter of the Master of this ship are purely co-incidental.'

When I lived in Point Piper in Sydney, I used to sail a lot at weekends with not stuffy but let's say strictly by-the-rules-'white-ensign-flying' yachtsmen. We would often rendez-vous in Pittwater and one day I spotted 'Sea Vixen' and said, 'Oh good, some chums of mine are here.' My host that day (Commander Hugh Eaton) said 'How can you possibly know these people? There is a television aerial on that Tupperware boat.' 'Yes,' I replied. 'They have a television set, every comfort, music and all mod-cons.' 'Sea Vixen' was, after all, Patsy's weekend cottage, and her amazing store cupboard on board supplied lots of other boats with delicious extras they had forgotten to bring. Whenever we were short of almost anything, over we would go in a dinghy to what we nicknamed Harrod's Food Hall. (Here I am exaggerating, of course … and perhaps going on too long.)

I have purposely not been chronological. Later we shall all be at Frank's golf club and talking about various fun times we have shared with Patsy, so going back a little …

I told how, when I lived in Paris, Patsy and Frank had once come to stay with me. Frank was on a busy business trip and I was working all day, so Patsy just took over my apartment at 33 avenue de Villiers. She did all the shopping, managed the maid, and made friends with the owners of the local charcuterie and boulangerie while not speaking a word of French. She just opened her purse, put the money on the counter and signalled them to take what she owed. The French adored her and told me they loved her smile. Incidentally, it was while the Foxes were with me that Lisa was conceived … born in Sydney, Australia, but started in Paris, France!

I concluded by saying:

let us all thank Almighty God for Patsy's life. She was a wonderful wife, a wonderful mother, a caring and dear friend whom we shall all miss. I hope that God will understand if she wants to re-arrange the decor in heaven, or fluff up the clouds as she used to fluff up cushions the minute after people had gone, or even change the rainbow to her favourite pastels and beige. Who knows, perhaps she will put up a few notices. If I could write one now it would be to repeat what the writer Alan Jay Lerner wrote when his friend Maurice Chevalier died in 1971: 'I envy the angels.'

Just as I had hesitated when Frank asked me to give Patsy's eulogy, I was very nervous when Jane Fraser of the *Australian* newspaper asked me to write an obituary for dear Kevin O'Neill at the beginning of 1997. 'I can't do that, I've never written one,' I pleaded. 'Oh yes, you can ... you were a friend of Kevin O'Neill and although obituaries have appeared written by newspaper journalists we want one by someone who knew him well.' It is difficult, almost impossible, to refuse Jane Fraser, so I sat down at my typewriter and composed my first obituary. Published on 9 January 1997 in our national newspaper, it said:

Kevin O'Neill, whose floral flair gave joy to thousands, died of cancer after a short illness on 4 January 1997. Not only for me, but for thousands of others, his passing will be a great sorrow, for he was a magical man. As Leo Schofield said on Tuesday 7 January 1997 in his eulogy at the Mass of Thanksgiving at St Ignatius Church in Richmond, Victoria, 'The collective loss is vast. For Kevin had friends and admirers not just in Melbourne, where he enjoyed the status of icon in the city, but throughout Australia and throughout the world.'

Born in Melbourne into a Salvation Army family, O'Neill made up his mind at an early age that flowers would be his life. He did his apprenticeship with John Holdsworth, at that time the best florist in Melbourne. After his training he went into business on his own, with his mentor's blessing. Later he worked for many luminaries, including Dame Zara Holt, and did arrangements for Dame Mabel Brookes as well as for the Packers and the Murdochs. He created a memorable arrangement for Paul Hogan's second wedding. The Queen once asked that photographs of a dinner party attended by Prince Charles be sent to her so she could see the floral centre pieces.

He also decorated for commercial ventures such as the much talked about and anticipated Spring Flower Shows at David Jones. Despite the many florists who attempted to emulate his style you always knew an O'Neill bouquet. It was just right. If you asked for something really simple as a gift it would be three perfect gardenias. His magic was not only through his incredible talent with flowers, plants and superlative ideas for lighting and decorating, it was his charm.

I quoted Schofield again: 'To Kevin everyone was special, no one person more important than another.' I reflected on how Kevin had helped so many of us raise money for good causes. When charity budgets were tight, he would suggest simple extras that would not cost much—lots of ivy, shiny leaves or twigs, green and red apples, and he would make the centre pieces look like a million dollars. What is more, he often generously donated everything and let us sell them to raise extra dollars. He seldom said no to a worthy cause.

The most outstanding church decoration I have ever seen was in a tiny church in England for the wedding of Gretel Packer [my goddaughter]. The entire walls were covered with cream, white and off-white flowers, most of them scented. It was O'Neill's attention to fine details that made him the best in the country. For example, if doing a country wedding, he would fly up to the house and photograph all the family vases. He would then plan the decorations of the marquee. Then, early on the day, the flowers would arrive and so would he. His brilliant arrangements would just be put directly into the vases. Hostesses were saved any worry whatsoever whenever O'Neill, John Graham (his partner of 35 years, and marketing manager) and caterer Peter Rowland were involved in any special occasion.

The other outstanding church decoration was, of course, at his own thanksgiving mass. There were in all 100 wreaths from friends, including many sent by the more famous people for whom he had worked: a wonderful tribute to a man whose flowers had provided so many with much joy. Even more moving were those done by all his staff and many who had worked with him over the years. These were a wonder of white with greenery. There were delphiniums, hydrangeas, many variations of lily, roses and peonies. In all there were eight huge arrangements forming a V near his coffin and the altar. One can only imagine the anguish and sorrow of the devoted staff. And, at the entrance to the church were the special and prized rare Lilium giganteums which were grown and nurtured by O'Neill in Mount Macedon where he lived.

O'Neill worked with much enthusiasm with John Truscott who designed the interior of the Victorian Arts Centre and Concert Hall and who won three Oscars for his costume and stage design. Together they started Botanica at the Melbourne International Festival and between them they gave the Arts Centre a sense of magic.

I ended my obituary by quoting Truscott: 'Kevin O'Neill is not only one of the most creative people in this town but he is also the nicest of men.'

Also the nicest of men, as well as one of the most visionary of people in this town, was Kenneth Myer AC DSO, who died on 31 July 1992, together with his wife when their plane crashed in Alaska.

Ken Myer and I were contemporaries. He was a few months younger than I and we had been friends since 1950, when I was the buyer for all the imported fashions and accessories at the Myer Emporium. Ken was doing his 'stage' in the coat department. He used to get me to buy the odd Paris or London couture garment for 'them' (coats and raincoats) to copy. He was a wonderful man even then, adored by the staff and the best looking guy there. We stayed chums, as I've said. I was never really a close friend of his first wife, but became a friend and admirer of Yasuka Myer, his second. John Truscott and I often made up a foursome for dinner or the theatre and when we heard of that tragic accident we both said that a worse tragedy would have been if they had not died together: no one could imagine one wanting to live without the other. It was the most amazing marriage of great love—never mind the difference in nationalities (Yasuka was Japanese).

I remember Ken's great qualities: his enormous ability to speak publicly without notes and to remember every single name or sponsor that had to be thanked or acknowledged; and his support for the arts, which was mammoth in generosity and in hands-on help. He was probably one of the best chairmen in the world, according to people who worked with him. I was always amazed at his modesty and self-effacement. He never forgot old friends. The Myer Emporium actually brought me out to Australia in 1949 and Ken always referred to me as 'their imported Pom'.

It was in 1962 that I first met Diana Vreeland; she was fashion editor of American *Vogue* in New York. I had just been appointed editor of Australian *Vogue* and was spending four weeks in the New York offices of Condé Nast Inc. I recall there was such a 'buzz' about 'DV' joining Vogue, as everyone guessed she was for the top job when dear old Jessica Daves resigned. For fashion excitement and influence in the 'rag trade' in those days, *Harper's Bazaar* was the leader and Diana Vreeland was *their* fashion editor. Condé Nast 'pinched' her—and were wise to do so, in the opinion of many of the staff, especially the more creative minded who were becoming slightly stifled by the formal way Vogue operated under Jessica. (She even used to wear her hat in the office!)

During many other visits to New York, and when visiting Paris to cover the couture collections for our *Vogue*, my admiration for DV grew and grew. Why? Partly because of her *enormous* contribution to fashion. She was the only woman in the business who *created* taste rather than followed it, partly because of her own individual elegance, partly because she was always so positive in encouraging talent. She was so helpful to me for nearly ten years.

She was very short-sighted (in the literal sense). I would put my head round the door of her leopard-pattern carpeted office and say 'Mrs Vreeland … it's Sheila from Australia'. 'Ah, the kangaroo editor,' she would say. 'Come on in. We are just co-ordinating accessories for these coats that will be photographed in Russia. Do you know the wonderful light in Leningrad?' I did not, unfortunately, but would sit in and learn more from her 'run-through' sessions with her fashion editors and the way she inspired them. At another session I remember her talking about locations for a group of winter clothes. She said to the photographer: 'I want them all in front of wonderful doors. You'll have to go to Europe … there are no really magnificent doors in America.' Gosh, how I envied her budget!

I was constantly amused at the way she gave one credit for knowing. 'Sheila, *you* know that the Duchess of Windsor invented the short evening dress?' No, I did not; I thought Cardin did. 'Well, *she* made it *smart*.' And DV went on to tell me about dinner parties with the Windsors in their house in the Bois de Boulogne. Then: 'Get someone in Australia to make something *smart*.'

She was incredibly helpful over advanced trends for colour—in fact, a genius with this, as our climates were reversed. There were six months between our winter and the Paris collections, so it was feasible for me to get our industries such as the textile and shoe people to know the right colours in good time. Diana was also a genius with her *descriptions* of colour. Years later, viewing the film *Russia House* which the brilliant director Fred Schepisi filmed on location in Leningrad, I recalled DV's descriptions of the special slightly pinkish light in what is now called St Petersburg, and the pale blue of the palaces. One of her descriptions, however, mystified Margaret Ingersoll, *Vogue*'s esteemed fabric editor, when I was there. 'Mrs Vreeland, I am afraid that the shade of blue you want is not on the market …' to which she got the reply: 'No Margaret, that is why it is so good.' While I personally did not hear her say it, her statement 'Pink is the navy blue of India' is known throughout the industry.

DV even invented beauty trends. Another time in New York she said to me, 'Sheila, *you* know the wonderful eyelashes on your kangaroos?' No, I could not truthfully say that I did! 'They go straight down like blinds. Do get one of your photographers to shoot one close up [with a camera] for me.' We did and the shot was published as a new idea for false eyelashes, which were 'in' in the 60s—and for which DV gave *Vogue* Australia the credit.

To me she always appeared to be pro-Australian while never having been here. Always happy to share any ideas that could be helpful to Australian *Vogue,* she would say 'Sheila, talk to Allene Talmay [her features editor] before you leave. She has Anthony Burgess writing a piece for us. He will let you "lift" it for very little.' Talmay would buy an author's United States rights for large fees, with an almost nominal one for poor young Australian *Vogue.* (This, incidentally, annoyed the hell out of British *Vogue*, who were obliged to negotiate for expensive European rights.) When I was covering the Paris collections, Vreeland's big car and chauffeur were made available to me day and night. Generously she would say, 'We must give a ride to the kangaroo editor' when I was rushing to the next showing. I was the only one without car and driver—my budget was so small. I always remember thinking that Vreeland's bills at the Hotel Crillon alone would exceed by thousands of dollars my entire colour budget for the whole year. American *Vogue* took a whole floor, installed an art department and studio for fashion editors to work '*sur place*' (on site) twenty-four hours a day for about ten days.

I envied Diana Vreeland, but adored her too. She was my mentor—stylish in the true sense of the word, with staggeringly high standards and attention to detail; hard working; generous, with impeccable manners. In addition, she showed great personal wisdom. Two sayings of hers will stay with me always. One was: 'I never remember anything unpleasant—remember that!' The other: 'Keep your secret. That's your power over others.'

Diana Vreeland to me was the only *genius* fashion editor. She even helped our own fashion industry. I should explain. A golden rule with my staff when travelling overseas was that they must *promise* me that, whenever they visited other Condé Nast offices, they would wear Australian-made clothes (needless to say, I obeyed this rule myself). DV often commented: 'Your young lot when they come over always look so healthy and energetic and they seem so proud of what they're wearing.' She often requested the name of the designer of the garment that took her eye, which resulted in some very young Australian designers (Trent Nathan was one) being introduced to the United States market.

Diana Vreeland died in August 1989. Indeed, I envy the angels.

**9**

Good judgement comes from experience ... and experience comes from bad judgement.

**(I have written this on the flyleaves of my diaries over many years but cannot remember who said it. I think it was my mother.)**

# Disappointments
# and Other Disasters

When I returned to Melbourne from living in London, in 1980, Ita Buttrose decided not to continue with the Sheila Scotter page I had been writing for the *Women's Weekly* for four and a half years. (Incidentally, the magazine was published weekly then—which means, if my sums are correct, that I must have written 234 pieces.) Naturally I was disappointed. But I quite understood that she already had staff who could write about local personalities and their lifestyles, and as I no longer lived overseas and my page had been running for so long, it was time for a change.

Time for a change for me, too. I studied the newspaper scene in Victoria and was rather impressed by the weekly 'Melbourne Living' section in the *Age*. I thought, why not have a go? I have never actually *applied* for a job; I have always been approached—even when I lacked the relevant experience. In dreaming up a job for myself at the *Age*, I came the closest ever to applying.

Through a friend, Claude Forell, one of the senior writers at the *Age*, an interview was arranged with Creighton Burns, then editor of the paper. I will admit to being slightly scared of meeting him. I had never written for a newspaper, and was not a member of any union. But it seems he had either read or heard about my page in the *Women's Weekly*;

when I started sort of 'selling' myself and some ideas for a short column, he cut the interview short with a charming 'When can you start?'

My brief was to report and give opinions on anything I found interesting or new in fashion, beauty, entertaining, travel, fashions in living, even food ... you name it. This column ran for five years and I really enjoyed writing it. As described by Stephen Downes, editor of the whole Tuesday section, 'Melbourne Living' was 'A vital dynamo in the machine of the city's buying patterns.'

I realised (with some pride) that my column was widely read. Not just because I received numerous personal letters from readers and recipients of editorial mentions of products, services, places and so on. But more importantly (to me) because the *Age* research staff told me that enquiries for information on past items were second in number to those received concerning Beverley Sutherland Smith's much-loved culinary page. Of course, I was second by quite a long margin as Beverley was deservedly one of Australia's most popular cookery writers. She wrote for the *Age* for twenty years. Goodness knows why they ever let her go, but I accept the fact that editors are entitled to make changes. *However*, I must admit that I was disappointed when a new editor was appointed to 'Melbourne Living'; he decided to let *me* go! Disappointed yes, but comforted by the letter I received from that gentleman of editors, Creighton Burns, who wrote:

Dear Sheila
Steve Harris tells me he has talked to you recently about his feeling that it is time to draw the line on

your column. I understand his reasons and agree with him. Columns in newspapers rarely manage to survive more than a few years—as you will know better than most, as a result of your earlier experiences.

I write now to thank you for your help over the last five years. I know your column interests many readers and I am sure many of them will be sad to see you go. I hope your new ventures prosper and that you will remember us with as much affection as we remember you. Thank you again.

Yours Creighton

About three years before I left the *Age* (it must have been 1982), I was approached by an American/Sydney friend Dwane McHolick who was the advertising, promotion and visual merchandise director of David Jones Australia. He asked me whether I would consider writing an unusual column for their advertising department. He had this idea of an editorial-type column running down the right-hand side of DJ's full page advertisements. I was hesitant at first because of my association with the *Age*. 'We do not want to use your name,' he said. 'It is your taste. I want you to select personally four or five items each week, describe them in your own way, giving price details and where they can be found in the Melbourne store. What do you say?'

The fee offered was three times what they paid me at 'Melbourne Living'. I wanted to accept but only if this was acceptable to Creighton Burns. It was. He gave me his permission and I gave him my solemn word that David Jones would not receive special treatment in my own by-lined column. They never did. Nor were they neglected, but because I was so careful I think that Myer and Georges might have been advantaged!

In his day McHolick was one of the most brilliant creative retail executives I knew, always thinking up exciting new ways to sell merchandise. At his suggestion I ended the so-called 'Potpourri' column with two or three lines of 'Applause'. This had nothing to do with anything in the store, but was praise for something in the arts, something achieved by sportsmen and -women, perhaps something new in the city of Melbourne, or in regional Victoria. The idea was copied by others, and who could blame them? It was a very successful merchandising concept, with valuable sales figures to prove it.

In my weekly column in 'Melbourne Living' in the *Age* on Tuesday 4 June 1985 I wrote:

Last week I attended the glamorous black-tie opening of Melbourne's newest department store. Briefly I tell you that Figgins Diorama of Collins Street (directly opposite Georges) is absolutely spectacular.

It is an exciting concept in retailing that will definitely be a smash hit with those fortunate enough to possess both money and good taste. But, in my opinion, Figgins Diorama will do for Melbourne, Victoria, what Neiman-Marcus did for Dallas, Texas, many years ago.

People came to Dallas from all over the world, enticed by the exceptionally high standard of fashion merchandise and the wondrous ways it was displayed, packaged and promoted at NM. They still do. So, thank you Mr Figgins, for lifting the standards here in marvellous Melbourne. I salute you, and wish everyone in your Diorama great success.

Later that day Dwane McHolick telephoned me from Sydney saying that he had some shattering news. 'I have just hung up from Brian Walsh who is in Adelaide today and who asked me whether I had read your column in Tuesday's *Age*.' Dwane told him yes, he had, to which Brian said, 'Well, did you see what she wrote about that new store? You can fire her. I won't have anyone employed by David Jones writing favourable things about potential competition.'

I knew that Brian Walsh was inclined to be vindictive and arrogant, but he was the managing director of all the David Jones Group of stores, and he was Dwane's boss. I asked Dwane 'What did you say to that?' and he told me his answer: 'Listen Brian, this woman is a highly respected reputable journalist and obviously her job is to report and give her opinion on any new fashion development in Melbourne.' Walsh said, 'I don't give a damn, just fire her.'

Poor Dwane sounded very upset. There was nothing he could do and I felt sorry for him. Me? I just felt absolutely furious with Brian Walsh. Dwane begged me to try to see Brian, who was due in the Regent Hotel, Melbourne, the following evening.

'He is known for flying off the handle. With your usual charm you could get him to change his mind.'

'No I won't do that. Stuff him. It is bloomin' DJ's loss,' said I immodestly.

He agreed. We both knew the commercial success of the 'Potpourri' column over three years.

'Well, will you write him a letter?'

'No, I won't do that either,' I said. 'But I'll write *you* one with a copy to the so-and-so.'

I composed what I think was a pretty good letter. It was, of course, written (as one might say) 'at' Walsh, to give him a let-out if he was sensible enough to take it.

My dear Dwane

I am sorry you had the unpleasant task of passing on Brian Walsh's sudden decision that he no longer wishes me to contribute towards the success of David Jones. His reaction (overreaction?) to a mention of Figgins Diorama in my AGE column of June 18 quite puzzles me. I refuse to believe that he would actually condemn someone for their professional integrity.

I have nothing but pride for what I have done for you and DJ's (Melbourne) during the last three years. My personal selection of merchandise, and the way my writing sells it has made POTPOURRI a bottom-line profitable success operation. Over and above the call of duty, I have enjoyed being a confidential and reliable negotiator, a totally discreet adviser and loyal friend. (Shall remain the latter always, whatever happens.)

I concede that I am not over popular with RT who has resented any criticism, however justified. But I certainly have the respect, admiration, even gratitude of the buyers, controllers and staff (with the exception of a few f ... wits!!) and I know you know this.

Through the Sheila Scotter column in the AGE, DJ's and Georges stores have received considerable promotional help and numerous editorial credits. They will continue to do so. As one of the country's most respected journalists I am not only entitled, but

expected, to comment on a new exciting addition to the retail scene in Melbourne. All I can say is 'APPLAUSE ... for any gentleman big enough to change his mind. There is no other store like David Jones ... and there is no other consultant like Sheila Scotter.'
Yours ever
Sheila

I sent a copy of this letter, together with a personal note, to every controller, fashion director and top buyer and to many senior sales staff at DJ's with whom I had worked so harmoniously and who I knew liked or respected me. I did consider leaking it to the press, but thought better of it. So this is the first time it has been published.

Needless to say Walsh was not a big enough man to change his mind. So Dwane had to carry out his boss's instructions and I was fired.

I remember reading somewhere 'Don't think people at the top have all the answers. They don't' ... and thinking, how jolly true.

Nearly nine years later I was approached by David Jones to join them again. Rod Mewing was then managing director of all the David Jones stores, and what they offered interested me. I accepted at once. Skye Macleod, their publicity manager at the time, put out the following press release:

David Jones Australia are pleased to announce the appointment of Sheila Scotter as a roving 'Ambassador' for our Victorian Division effective April 5, 1994.

Miss Scotter, who was formerly editor of *Vogue* Australia, will be an adviser to David Jones and use her wealth of experience gained from her roles in magazines, newspapers, fundraising, and the arts. Miss Scotter will be of great benefit to David Jones in anticipation of our expansion in the Victorian market.

The press release then included a statement from me:

I am thrilled that the directors of David Jones appreciate experience. You cannot create it, you must undergo it. During all my long working life I have been a contributor of ideas and influenced consumers of all age groups in fashion, retail and publishing scenes in Australia. This is a bold experiment for David Jones and one that I am sure will be beneficial for all concerned.

I must say I was rather pleased with my statement, until I read somewhere that Oscar Wilde had said 'Experience is the name people give their mistakes!'

The press release went on to chronicle my career thus far, all of which you have read about elsewhere in this book.

Well, I thought, a lot is going to depend upon my being accepted by the management of the Melbourne store. The appointment was certainly an unusually bold move by Rod Mewing, and the reasoning was obvious. The Sydney store had a very high profile in New South Wales. Their fashion parades, cosmetic and perfume launches were stylish and exciting and as a result always well patronised by fashionable society plus leading movers and shakers and other celebrities. They were extremely well covered by the newspapers, television news, and the glossy magazines. Skye Macleod was respected and did a terrific job. The in-store cocktail parties to launch the beginning of each winter and summer collection were considered important social occasions in Sydney. Sad to say, this was not the case with the Melbourne store, and in my role as 'ambassador at large' I was to rectify the situation.

I thoroughly enjoyed doing the job. Fortunately the general manager in Melbourne, Tim Quinn, and I got on famously. He gave me almost complete freedom. We had fortnightly meetings (one to one) in which I could discuss or criticise ideas for stylish improvements without fear of offending any particular controller or buyer who had different views.

At the time (1994) DJ's in Bourke Street had quite an elegant restaurant which provided rather good food, at sensible prices, with silver service, attentive staff, and a plus factor: *no* music. Here I could (and did) host lunches for important potential customers, fashion loving friends, and certain selected press, most of whom were unaware of its existence. All gave it high praise and often returned, bringing others into the store, which of course was the point of the exercise.

It was, I remember, a pleasure working with the then manageress, Simone Boileau, and her staff who seemed to enjoy lifting their game for certain events that required much more than the call of duty. I recall the chef being given special praise by members of the Columnists' Club when we held a lunch in this restaurant on the third floor. (Incidentally, this club for journalists was founded in 1982 by Claude Forell, Ross Campbell and myself, and it is still going strong.)

At the time DJ's were very generous in their support of the arts, and we had great fun arranging a farewell tea party for the children (all from Melbourne) performing in the Australian Opera's (and Benjamin Britten's!) *Midsummer*

*Night's Dream.* They were departing the next day for the Edinburgh Festival. We engaged a magician to entertain the children and at the same time held a champagne party for their parents in an adjacent room.

Tim Quinn was thrilled when I persuaded Dame Elisabeth Murdoch to open the Kevin O'Neill Spring Flower Show that year, and to stay for a luncheon in her honour, again *in* the store. I told him that I was most anxious to invite only people who would interest *her*. 'Go for it,' he said. 'Don't inflict too many retailers on her.' Extra crowds came not only to see the glorious floral displays but also to see and hear the Dame.

Two stylish personalities who caused a few heads to turn when they entered this restaurant were Miss Maina Gielgud AO, then artistic director of the Australian Ballet, and Mr Noel Pelly AM, the former administrator and now on the Ballet Board. They came to the store late morning for the signing of Noel's book *Zita*, which told the fascinating story of Maina's Hungarian-born aristocratic mother, Zita Gordon Gielgud. In the book department on the ground floor both Noel and Maina signed copies galore, seated together at an elegant black table adorned with red roses (the table, not them!) They then enjoyed a delicious lunch in the restaurant with me and Dennis Biggs, who was the merchandise controller of DJ's ground floor.

There was also a gallery in the Bourke Street store, on the second floor. Although not large it was an adequate space for all sorts of exhibitions—paintings, sculpture, photography, historic costumes and jewellery—which attracted all kinds of people who may not have been into the store before.

To reach the gallery they had to walk through the fashion departments—which, in my opinion, meant that the gallery was good public relations for new customers.

I recall the great success of one exhibition that attracted literally hundreds and hundreds of people. We co-operated with the Melbourne International Festival and Diane Masters who organised the Hall Ludlow Couturier Retrospective exhibition in 1994. This elegant former high fashion model, and close friend of Hall Ludlow (and myself), did all the research and, with help from the visual merchandising staff of DJ's, put on the first retrospective fashion show by a living Australian designer. Diane and I hosted the opening and spoke together, giving background information on Ludlow plus a special message from one of his favourite customers, Mrs Loti Smorgon, who was overseas at the time. For two weeks Ludlow made himself available each morning to talk to the many visitors who came to see the 1950s and 60s creations by this great couturier. In some cases women were looking at themselves in the past, for we had been lent wedding and bridesmaid dresses, going-away outfits, and ball gowns from both mothers and daughters who were former clients at Hall Ludlow's salon in Collins Street, Melbourne.

When needed, and sometimes liaising with Skye Macleod's Sydney office, I would act as hostess for certain press launches, such as the opening of the Fortnum & Mason section in the Food Store. Then there were overseas VIPs constantly visiting the store to promote or check up on their products. One of the most popular, and for me the most fun as she was a close friend of many years, was Carol Phillips. Formerly the dynamic managing editor of American *Vogue*,

Carol was probably the most highly respected beauty editor of all time. Certainly, the Estée Lauder company considered her so: they enticed her to join them, to create from scratch a new line, Clinique. I remember her saying to me in New York, 'I am quite sad to be leaving Vogue after all these years, but I am going to be solvent at last!' (Hard working executives in the cosmetic industry earned far more than hard working editors of glossy magazines.) Carol Phillips ended up as chairman of Clinique and this was her first trip to Australia.

Part of my job, I felt, was to give backup and guidance to the young girls assigned to do 'public relations' for the David Jones Melbourne store. In my opinion they were underpaid and overworked and so there were quite a few changes in this department. However, all went well for nearly fourteen months. I helped raise the standard of in-store promotions and, through personal contacts, provided many more appropriate names to add to the 'A' list for invitations to the more important events and fashion parades in the store.

But then came a sudden and total change of top management in Sydney. Rod Mewing was fired and one Chris Tideman from the UK appointed managing director in his place. Inevitably there were policy changes, and the sacking (I should say retrenchment) of loyal, experienced controllers and buyers. A Mr Martin McRobert was put in charge of DJ's Melbourne. Personally I had not heard of him in the retail scene. He was brought down from Parramatta. Obviously he was obliged to carry out Tideman's directions if he wished to keep his job, and while I quite liked the man I had no respect for him.

I soon decided to leave David Jones. When I went to see Mr McRobert with my letter of resignation I couldn't help feeling he was somewhat relieved! On 28 May 1995 two items appeared in the local press. The headlines amused me. Lawrence Money's 'Spy' column in the *Sunday Age* announced: 'DJ's Duchess storms out' and continued:

'I'm bored with it,' says silver duchess Sheila Scotter, who rattled the crockery at David Jones' store by quitting as consultant and ambassador-at-large. It was a characteristically no-nonsense exit for one of the matriarchs of the local social set.

'The store is being run from Sydney. It is not going the way I think it should but you can't argue against things. I don't need the hassles.'

DJ's Victorian chief, Martin McRobert, told Spy: 'It is a shame Sheila is so critical. We had a good relationship. I have my feet firmly on the ground in Melbourne. We are a different company than we were several years ago. Much more focussed.'

(Perhaps I should explain that Peter Janson of Rutherglen House gave me my nickname of Silver Duchess years ago. I don't dislike it!)

In the Sunday *Herald Sun* the headline was 'DJ rover moves on' and the article said:

Voguish Sheila Scotter has resigned as consultant and ambassador at large for David Jones. 'My forte is stylish promotion,' she said, 'and that's not happening so much any more. And when it does happen, it emanates from the new management team in Sydney.'

General Manager of the Melbourne store, Martin McRoberts [sic] said 'We sat down and discussed the future. I think it doesn't only lie with so-called high society. Until my arrival most management decisions for Melbourne came from Adelaide. Now there is somebody on the ground here so I can direct things personally. It was an amicable arrangement, Sheila is now free to pursue other interests without being tied strictly to David Jones. And we shall certainly call on her.'

He didn't. I still kept in touch with what was going on, and was a weekly client of their Hair and Beauty salon (still am—it is very well run and Albert is a gentle genius with hair).

A few months after I left I was contacted by a leading journalist from the *Sydney Morning Herald* and asked for my opinion on what was going wrong with David Jones. My comments referred mainly to the Melbourne store and the running of it, although I also knew the Sydney store quite well. In a fax dated 5 October 1995, I said:

In hindsight I think the major mistake was made by Rod Mewing by not grabbing Robert Hampson to be Merchandise Director when he returned from the United States and England ... he was the (DJ's) merchandise director before he left Sydney ... very successful and highly thought of but Rod Mewing may have considered him a rival! I admire and like Rod Mewing very much but feel this was foolish and that if he had done this the present English management and fashion direction would not have eventuated. (Anyone could check up on Hampson's record at Harrods and the whole House of Fraser group etc from ex-DJ's people such as Dwane McHolick.)

Regarding the new English management, I know Mr Tideman likes people who can talk research and marketing jargon but to me retailing should be a hands-on relationship between customers and suppliers.

Sydney's fashion needs, for example, are quite different from Melbourne's. People dress differently, the climate is different and the taste, too, in my opinion. It seems to people in Melbourne that the new Sydney management does not particularly want to meet customers or suppliers (this is what I hear frequently as a complaint). They pop down for a day only and while I know accountants are essential to the business they cannot <u>run</u> retail stores ... costings, budgets and forecasts etc are vital but experienced good merchandise directors and their buyers are the key to <u>profit.</u> They have sacked so many experienced loyal controllers and buyers from the Melbourne store (I gather in Sydney, too, but you can find this out) and have put youngsters in with not much idea of <u>service</u>. But of course the cost in salaries is perhaps what they want on the bloomin' bottom line!??

I said that I had adored working under Rod Mewing and the Sydney crowd when I was a consultant to the store as their ambassador-at-large but soon realised it was not going to work with this new lot, who seemed in my opinion to be 'down-grading' in every way.

Promotions were no longer going to be done in style (again <u>my</u> opinion). I do have praise for some of the development of their own DJ's label which Mrs Tideman has done in the fashion departments but I am not impressed with their advertising, which used to be great and is now no comparison to Myer. (I am talking of the fashion ads in newspapers: the catalogues are still quite good.)

The traditional Spring Flower Show this season (September) was so disappointing compared with previous glorious displays by Kevin O'Neill. They even brought someone down from Sydney to do the flowers this year! Quite a lot of Melbournians were disappointed and said so, but again it was a cost cutting exercise I am told. However, as Kevin O'Neill Florist is incidentally <u>in</u> the Bourke Street store why not promote his shop within their own store? Talking of advertising, for example … here in the Age newspaper they had a column called 'Houndstooth News' and this column used to have a houndstooth check border. Now it has a funereal black border which seems crazy to me when the DJ's graphic design on shopping bags etc. is so well known. It seems they do not want any <u>traditional</u> David Jones … hope they are right but am darn sure they are not!!

The *Sydney Morning Herald* article was published on 11 October 1995. Alas, my comments were not quoted (due to a space problem, I was told, which I fully understand can happen from time to time). However, two years later I re-read what I had faxed and, if you will forgive my immodesty, I thought I was pretty spot on … in hindsight?

My sadness about what was happening to this once great retailer in Melbourne was shared by a good many others. Sales were falling and shares had slumped to an all time low, yet still this English CEO did not appear to be at all interested in listening to any local advice. As to what happened to Georges of Collins Street (under DJ's direction) … well, in my opinion they killed it.

I well remember when, back in 1983, Brian Walsh (then DJ's CEO) appointed Susan Baggie, his top fashion controller of the whole group, as merchandise director of Georges. The store then was often compared (as I did with Figgins) to the famous Neiman-Marcus of Dallas, Texas—not for its profit margins, but for its special position in the retail market, its quality merchandise, and the excellent service of highly trained staff. Susan became a close friend. She still is, in spite of the difference in our ages. I myself had worked for Georges as their high fashion buyer, way back in the 1950s, and we have often discussed together the 'death' of this gem of a store. Recently, in a conversation that I happen to have a record of, Susan summed up her thoughts:

Shopping in Collins Street was a very special experience. It was the combination of carefully selected merchandise from around the world, presented in an environment that complemented the goods and sold by staff who believed wholeheartedly in what they were doing. In expanding to Sydney, David Jones demonstrated they had no appreciation of what they owned. Taking some stock and pinning a name plate on some excess space in the David Jones city store was easy. Ignoring the special spirit and the environment of the Collins Street store, developed over 100 years, was fatal. Predictably the Sydney stores failed.

Like a spoilt child DJ's accepted no blame and turned on the Melbourne operation, treating it as a 'family embarrassment'. It stripped Georges of its most worthwhile assets—the international labels that had taken years to acquire—and bullied the Melbourne stores into fitting more neatly into the DJ family mould. Eventually Georges died, I am sure to the great relief of the David Jones management. The only greater embarrassment DJ's could have suffered would be to have someone take it over and make it successful again. There should be a brass plate on the Collins Street site: 'In memory of Georges. Brought to an end by people who knew the cost of everything, and the value of nothing.

I think she is right but am happy to know that the name of this wondrous store will live again in Collins Street.

I am also particularly happy that, under the current

Australian management of the David Jones Group, the Melbourne DJ's store is once again looking stylish and exciting visually, and I hear trading figures are on the increase. Since part of my career was involved with the buying and selling of clothes, I have never lost my fascination with leading department stores both in Australia and overseas. As a shopper I certainly appreciate the convenience of two great retail stores, Myer and DJ's, alongside each other in the Bourke Street Mall.

---

When I started my career in the fashion world as a model, I was working for a while at Spectator Sports. The boss, a rather ill-tempered man known by his surname, Wallace, was not easy to work for and this was my first job. When Christian Dior came out with his New Look in 1947, Wallace created a separate collection of more expensive glamour clothes in this new elegant length. After the war we were all so fed up with dull skimpy looks and just adored the full skirted, calf length dresses, nipped in jackets and cinched waists that were going to change the whole world of fashion. Everyone copied Dior.

As models, we were allowed to borrow the odd sample from the collection—naturally only with permission. At short notice one evening I was invited to dine and dance at The Savoy Hotel. I wanted to stun my friends by wearing a divine black velvet dinner dress, which had been made on me and was my favourite from the Wallace Collection. The boss was not available. No one else could give permission. I borrowed it. During the evening, as I was sitting at a table in The Savoy, a note was brought over to me. It read: 'That is a charming dress you are wearing, Sheila. Do come and see me in the morning.' I looked round, and saw Wallace with a party of friends on the other side of the ballroom. I was convinced I would be fired the following day but the old boy was in a good mood ... so he admitted. I like to think I was such a good model that he could not sell clothes without me!

---

Jean Scotter, my cousin-in-law, was on the committee of the Army Benevolent Fund in the UK and involved in the organisation of a large fundraising fair at the Dorchester Hotel in London. I was asked to help out on the Tombola stall. Each year Her Majesty the Queen attends and spends quite a while visiting various stalls; it is just luck if she stops to talk or buy something. I was up front at our table of prizes with a smart sergeant in charge of the barrel containing the tickets. He would roll the barrel, someone would put their hand in and draw out a numbered ticket, and I would have to find the corresponding number on one of the prizes. We had hundreds of them. I hasten to say that I did not have anything to do with the detailed organisation, otherwise the numbered prizes would have been placed in groups: tickets 1 to 50, 50 to 100 and so on, instead of all over the place. So what do you think happened? Yes, you've guessed it, the Monarch was approaching with her Lady in Waiting, who bought her a ticket; the royal hand pulled out number 132! Do you think I could find the wretched prize? Minutes went by, the sergeant was getting nervous, I was not exactly calm. And then I thought, 'Oh well I'll just have to cheat.' I picked up a big white teddy, which happened to be number 104, and presented it to Her Majesty. 'Oh what luck. I shall give it to Anne,' she said. I chose it knowing the Princess was expecting a baby, but was terrified that the next person would pull out 104, having witnessed what I had done. It was an awkward moment.

---

During my time as vice-chairman of the Victoria State Opera Foundation, I organised, with the help of a panel of judges headed by Leo Schofield, the Dame Joan Hammond Award. Since 1986, under the auspices of the Foundation, the award has been presented annually to the person who has made the greatest contribution to opera in Australia during the previous year, or an outstandingly important contribution over a period of years. We held the presentation dinners in various capital cities, and in 1992 it was held at the Hilton Hotel, Brisbane, on 25 September, in the presence of Her Excellency, Leneene Forde, Governor of Queensland. What should have been a truly enjoyable evening turned out to be a bitter disappointment.

Dame Joan and I were in fact extremely annoyed at some changes made in Melbourne without our knowledge. Her letter of 30 September 1992 to the then chairman of the VSOF, Mr Peter Griffin, with an open copy to me, says it all:

Dear Mr Griffin

This will, I regret to say, be more of a questionnaire than a letter. Since you became Chairman of the Foundation I have been ignored. It would have been a courtesy to have advised me that the format of the Dame Joan Hammond Award was to be changed. Since the inception of this Award the Chairman, Mr David Gibbs, consulted with me and kept me informed of any pertinent matters.

One of my prime rules must have been changed in order that a member of the [Company] could be elected the 1992 winner! Who could have persuaded a man of such integrity, Ken Mackenzie-Forbes, to have accepted, and place himself in such an ignominious position?

For the first time I could not emit surprise when revealing the name of the winner, as had been customary. The day before the Award dinner I received a letter from the VSO. It contained a large sheet of paper which contained the word 'MEDIA' around the edges. On it was, to my surprise, the name of the winner and giving his very interesting curriculum vitae. In heavy print at the top it stated that it was EMBARGOED etc, etc. This made it rather theatrical.

Why was I not informed that you were to give a vote of thanks to the Donors? Your speech, in fact, became a duplication of mine. This could easily have been avoided.

It was very embarrassing when people asked you why so-and-so had not won the Award, giving you ample and very justified reasons why [they should have]. You placated them by saying not to worry as so-and-so will be the winner next year! What an indictment!

Two gentlemen said in my presence that the Award was so patently 'cooked' and it was a farce. I could not disagree.

It was a humiliating experience. I felt a sense of shame that the Award had been reduced to such a level of discussion.

I feel, in this instance, my name has been tarnished.
Yours sincerely
Joan Hammond

I, too, was bitterly disappointed to see that this prestigious award had been, to use Joan's words 'reduced to such a level of discussion.' My disappointment was deepened not only because a group of us had worked hard to promote its high standard, but also on behalf of the hundreds of generous people, both private and corporate, who had supported it financially for ten years.

Three days before the gala presentation of the award in Brisbane, I myself received telephone calls from local people who had said they had heard that the winner this year was Ken Mackenzie-Forbes (originally from Brisbane) and could they still get seats. One, incidentally, was his sister ... So for me, too, the 1992 dinner was a misfortune.

Another disaster was to come. After Dame Joan had been interviewed on the ABC's '7.30 Report', she received an astonishing letter from Sir Rupert Hamer, dated 1 July 1993, which she showed me. Both of us wondered whether it had been written by someone else—the aggressive tone was so un-Dick-Hamer-like, and the signature was such a long way down from the last paragraph, which read: 'Instead you have chosen to denigrate the Company publicly and ignore its achievement, and we all find that inexplicable.'

I witnessed Dame Joan's extreme distress, also her anger. It took her a long time to compose her reply, which was eventually written on 17 August 1993. She gave me a copy. On the matters she raised in the letter, Dame Joan and I could be said to speak with one voice; after years of voluntary work, I too had experienced ungracious behaviour from certain (paid!) members of the company. For this reason, I believe Dame Joan's incisive and important letter—another secret I have kept till now—should be published.

Dear Sir Rupert
It is because of my deep, sincere respect for you that I have delayed replying to your letter of 1st July 1993. As you'll know, I was connected with the Company long before I became Artistic Director. I became interested in it as an amateur group. From the moment of my first association with the then Victorian Opera Company, I have always maintained the deepest commitment to the well-being of the Company. It has been, and will always be, a most meaningful part of my life. You assert that I have now publicly denigrated the Company and further there is a hint that you are all so disappointed in me that you now regret naming the magnificent rehearsal studio after me. Such a quick and bitter reaction is very deplorable, and knowing and

admiring you as I do, I quite frankly find it difficult to believe that you could have written such a letter.

I never saw the '7.30 Report' on the ABC but I have had many interesting and supportive comments, including some from people close to and with a keen understanding of the Company. You must have been in a similar situation on many occasions when a report/interviewer asked a lot of questions and you had to reply off-the-cuff. One remark I repeated three times was that the VSO 'must not be allowed to die: it must live!'. That statement, so I believe, was snipped out by those who cut down the interview, and I am clearly compromised by the action.

I spoke honestly and openly to the ABC reporter, just as I try to be candid at all times. Although I understand that my comments were isolated and made to look as though I was refuting those of you and Ken Mackenzie-Forbes, believe me when I say that I was completely unaware of what anybody else had said to this person.

I received a very laudable and never-to-be-forgotten lesson when I first accepted a position on a Board. The number one rule is that the Board is responsible for everything, no matter what. Perhaps the VSO Board was unable to respond better because it was not sufficiently informed by management, but it is my firm belief that when there is a problem, for whatever internal or external reason, those responsible must be seen to be accountable. Had I still been on the Board at the time of this present crisis, I would have felt compelled to tender my immediate resignation in acknowledgement of this responsibility.

The recession has had to be accommodated by everyone, individuals and arts organisations alike, and I, at no time, was critical of individual members of the Board and Management, so many of for whom, including yourself, Jack Kennedy, Dame Margaret Guilfoyle and Alfred Ruskin, I have only admiration. I am aware of the ills and shortcomings of other companies, but surely, as we have all been adversely affected by this recession for some years, it would have been prudent for the VSO in recent years to work doubly hard at lowering production costs and introducing ways of selling tickets that better took account of the harsh economic climate. Aiming at the highest artistic standards is entirely commendable, but a greatly reduced income surely means that standards have to be re-negotiated in the light of the Company's inability to pay. It is easy to expand and very difficult to contract; but contracting now and building again later is what the Company must do.

I am afraid your letter was also very ill-timed for me. Lolita Marriott had died suddenly on 23rd June 1993. Incredibly the VSO, the Company to which I remain most devoted and with which I am most closely associated in the public eye, was the only company not to send a letter of condolence or some token of regret. Forget your anger with me, Lolita was one of your oldest and most loyal supporters, and this dismissal of her memory is both unwelcome and unworthy.

It has been saddening not to receive invitations to this year's VSO activities, and from the tone of the letter I have received, I take it to mean I am unwelcome to share in the Company's future. Your final paragraph explains the 'cut-off' to me of invitations to first-nights at the opera or any other nights at VSO functions, but I have to say that where you may have found my behaviour inexplicable, I find this response churlish.

The hostility of your response is incomprehensible to me and I am so disheartened to reach the twilight only to have this nightmare ending. Time has quenched all ire but a wound remains.

Yours sincerely

Joan Hammond

---

And now a disappointment to end all disappointments (it could also be called a disaster!). Some people will tell you that there is no such thing as bad publicity. I most certainly do not agree. To find my photograph and name in headlines on the front page of the tabloid newspaper *Truth*, on Saturday 7 November 1992 was, to say the least, a bitter disappointment. Disaster was to follow when other press and magazines followed, with their own accounts of an embarrassing confrontation that had taken place during a polo match at Werribee Park, Victoria the previous Sunday.

For the record, I can provide a ball-by-ball description of what really did happen. This is possible because my solicitor asked me at the time to type out an account of events in the form of a play script, recounting each person's words faithfully ...

Date: Sunday 1st November 1992
Venue: A round table for eight in the Grand Hyatt marquee at the polo at Werribee Park, Victoria
Occasion: Lunch
Those present: Douglas Butler, Harry M Miller, Diana Fisher, John Mackinnon, June McCallum and her nephew Andrew Broadbent (young), Sheila Scotter—all friends who wanted to sit together, and who knew each other (with the exception of Andrew Broadbent), all having fun and pulling each other's legs and joking a lot.
The episode: Up came Lillian Frank wearing a gold cowboy's hat. She came to the table to say hello (uninvited). The conversation went like this:

HARRY MILLER Where is Richard, Lillian?

LILLIAN FRANK He is home on his own. He likes to have some peace and quiet, he tells me.

SHEILA (definitely joking) Oh are you sure he does not have someone with him, Lillian? There was an item in the gossip column today.

LILLIAN Whose column?

SHEILA Lawrence Money's in the *Age*. Didn't you see it? (still obviously joking and people giggling a bit)

LILLIAN You are joking, Sheila.

SHEILA No, go and get a copy.

HARRY Yes, and Lillian you realise that I am his agent if there is any divorce. Sorry, I cannot act for you both. But if there is a book in it I will take you both on for the book!

All of this was said totally in joking format. Frank left the table and returned to where she was sitting. No abuse from her then. Most at the table had heard the whole conversation. We can only surmise that someone said later 'You could make a fuss and sue.' It was a Peter Ford who actually telephoned *Truth* (so I was told by the then editor Ian Dougal). He also telephoned the TV station Channel 10, and possibly the *Australian* newspaper and the *Telegraph/Mirror* (I cannot prove the last two.) Frank is very publicity seeking and well-known for it.

Two of my friends, Dulcie Boling and Sonia McMahon, are not very happy with Frank's behaviour. When Lillian Frank realised that she had had her leg pulled (or had been goaded on by a friend or friends) she abused me as I left the marquee to watch the polo. Very loudly she said, 'You are a bitch, Sheila Scotter. You are a bitch.'

No other conversation was heard by the public. Dulcie Boling tried to calm her down. I joined them and when I implied that she had come to our table uninvited, and why make such a fuss?, it was then that Frank said 'Who do you think you are? The Queen of England?'

Frank said to Dulcie, 'I'm going to sue her for $100,000. She cannot afford that and she is going to pay', etc. etc.

The main point is that *I* never mentioned the word 'divorce'. *Harry M did*, jokingly (as reported).

Inevitably there was an exchange of solicitors' letters. The last letter was from my solicitors, Kevin Minotti. It read:

*To Messrs Corrs Chambers Westgarth (Solicitors)*
*From Kevin Minotti, Sydney*
*30 November 1992*
*Re: LILLIAN FRANK*

We act for Miss Sheila Scotter and have been handed a

copy of your letter of 24 November 1992. We advise as follows:-

(a) Our client is amazed that your client's recollection of the events which occurred on 1 November 1992 differs so greatly from both hers and the recollections of other persons who were present during the course of the luncheon referred to:-

(b) The allegations made by your client with regard to the words alleged to have been used by our client at a luncheon on 1 November 1992 are denied:-

(c) We note that your firm does not identify any cause of action your client may have against our client nor does your firm assert imputations that may arise from the words that your client alleges our client used on 1 November 1992:-

(d) Any allegation of malice is denied:-

(e) We note that your client asserts that she has been the subject of considerable publicity and that her family has been embarrassed by that publicity. To this regard we note that your client has not sought to reduce the amount of coverage provided by the press in respect of the incident at the luncheon on 1 November 1992. In fact all the publications of those events would indicate that your client has encouraged as much publicity as possible of her version of the events. When one takes into account your client's admission in various articles published that she is 'embarrassed for myself that I was so rude' and your client's conduct generally on 1 November 1992 and subsequently this view is confirmed. In the circumstances it would seem clear

that your client's own conduct both at the lunch on 1
November 1992 and thereafter has caused any alleged
embarrassment to her family:-

(f) We cannot identify any cause of action that
arises against our client even on your client's version,
which is denied, of the events that took place on 1
November 1992 nor can we identify any damages that
your client has suffered. Accordingly, the proposal
incorporated in the second last paragraph of your letter
[which was to apologise and have the matter dropped]
is rejected:-

(g) We note the comments in your letter that 'it has
been suggested to our client that you would be unable
to pay any substantial damages'. We further note that
this suggestion to your client must have occurred prior
to her making that statement in a public place on 1
November 1992 and regard that statement and other
matters said by your client on 1 November 1992 and
subsequently as being highly defamatory to our client
with malicious intent. In this regard our client reserves
her rights:-

(h) Any assertion that your client is distressed by
reason of the events which occurred on 1 November
1992 is, we respectfully submit, occasioned by her own
conduct.
Yours faithfully
K J Minotti & Co

As far as I am concerned, this letter ended the matter.

**10**

Commuters give the city its tidal restlessness, natives give it solidity and continuity; but the settlers give it passion.

**E B White**

# London, Paris,
# Sydney, Melbourne

I am in agreement with Mr (or Mrs) White, quoted opposite, though personally, as a settler, I cannot claim to have *given* passion to any city: I firmly believe that settlers become more passionate about certain cities than the natives. I am not talking about short visits of a few weeks, even months—like those I have paid to New York or Calcutta—but actually *living in* and experiencing the basics of everyday life that can either give one enormous pleasure or irritate over a period of years.

When I moved from Sydney to London in 1971 to join Revlon, I lived at the lower end of St James's Street near St James's Palace and Pall Mall. My *tiny* apartment was literally only a few steps away from two of London's most beautiful parks: the spacious, open Green Park with its expansive stretches of green, green grass and avenue of trees; and St James's Park, which was more like a large formal garden, with its immaculate flower beds, exotic shrubs and manicured paths that converged on a miniature lake. At each end of the lake there were island bird sanctuaries and fountains. I used to walk in one park or the other nearly every day—in winter always during daytime but in summer often when the sun was low in the sky, making elongated shadows of the trees, when a group of us would gather for a picnic supper. I feel as sorry for anyone who has not experienced the long gentle twilight of a summer's evening in England as I do for those who have never witnessed one of our Australian sunsets.

My apartment was so small (a weeny sitting room, weeny studio bedroom, galley type kitchen, and bathroom with the 'loo in it) that it meant thinking up a new way to entertain friends, especially visiting Australians. What I did was invite people for drinks and a trip to the theatre. The glass dining table seated only four comfortably (six was a crowd) so I would serve scrumptious smoked salmon sandwiches, some pop-in-the-mouth homemade sausage rolls (hot) and stuffed olives with drinks, then take my visitors to the theatre, most of which were within walking distance and only ten minutes away. I'd leave a big pot of soup in the oven so we had something to eat later with bread and cheese or fresh fruit. It seemed to work ... it *had* to! Two people in my kitchen was a crowd, but this way I could cope with six or eight, as long as I was organised.

The fact that I could get away with so much in such a tiny space was due to ingenious design by Lex Aitken, of international fame.

Number 73 St James's Street was right in the heart of what can only be described as gentlemen's club land ... White's, Boodle's, Brooks's, the Army and Navy, Carlton, Junior Carlton, the Athenaeum, Naval and Military, the Travellers', to name a few. Many gave reciprocal rights to men's clubs in Australia. In the English summer, especially, I would often bump into a visiting Aussie who would open the conversation with 'Oh and what are you doing in these parts, my dear?' My standard reply—'Actually I live here'—always seemed to surprise them. It surprised me sometimes. I felt so lucky to be living in this area of London.

General household shopping was a joy. I had the choice of two rather special grocers who were suppliers, or to use their term, purveyors, to Buckingham Palace and held the Royal Warrant as grocers to Her Majesty the Queen. That will suit me, I thought! One, the legendary world famous Fortnum & Mason, where the ground floor staff carry out their duties in morning coats, still exists. The other, Jacksons of Piccadilly, which was where I opened an account, alas closed a few years ago. Jacksons was a private company established 400 years ago. The atmosphere was rather like a grand old village shop, where they managed to make their least illustrious customer feel like royalty. As a regular I became friends with some of the staff. Waggish Cyril, who ran the fruit, vegetables and salad section, was a cricket enthusiast. He never got over my first visit. I had assumed that parsley and mint were free (they were in Australia in those days). For a long time, as I approached, I'd hear 'Ah 'ere comes the Aussie cricketing bird who expects the parsley for nothing.' More ribaldry took place during Test matches.

When funds were low or if I needed exercise I would walk to the Berwick Street market in Soho, especially on a Tuesday when the 'egg' lady was at her stall selling free range eggs, fresh farm butter and Welsh cheeses. I used to walk a lot and got to know this part of London pretty well.

I was fortunate, too, in having a choice of where to worship if in London during a weekend. While officially in the parish of the Wren-built St James's Church in Piccadilly, I often attended the 11.30am service in the Chapel Royal, which was next door. (I liked sleeping late on a Sunday … still do!) If the weather was good and I felt energetic, I'd walk across St James's Park to the Guards Chapel in Birdcage Walk. I have to confess that this was my favourite service, for instead of an organist playing for the hymns, the music was belted out by a military band of either the Scots, Irish, Welsh or Grenadier guards, who took it in turn. What is more, there was usually an interesting visiting preacher. The service ended around noon, so one could conveniently join other 'staying-in-town-this-weekend' chums for lunch in nearby Knightsbridge, or walk back across the park to what I used to call my village of St James's. Other weekends would be spent in the country, often in the New Forest with Vernon and Shirley Simmonds, whose cosy house in Burley is still regarded by these darling friends as my second home. I loved, too, going to my cousin Michael Bazeley who lives and farms in Southwick, near Fareham, in another lovely part of Hampshire.

In Paris, (to refer again to the wisdom of E B White) the natives certainly give each *quartier* (district) solidity and continuity, and as a Parisian settler between 1958 and 1962 I was passionate about the 17th arrondissement (borough). I lived in a fifth floor apartment at 33 avenue de Villiers, on the corner of Place Malsherbe. My sitting room window framed a constant view of Sacré-Coeur high up in distant Montmartre. Seen from afar this white basilica is quite magical in sunlight or moonlight: nearby it looks like a wedding cake. I was working hard as head of the marketing division for the American textile company Joseph Bancroft & Sons (of Wilmington, Delaware, USA) but my life was made easier for me through dear old Berthe, who came every day as '*bonne à tout faire*' (maid of all work); she not only pampered me but taught me quite a lot … how to make toast on a typical French cooking stove with no grill, how to make a delicate but delicious soup using the outside lettuce leaves when she observed with horror that I discarded them. (I still use her recipe and have never thrown out any lettuce leaves since!) She tried to turn me into a more frugal shopper when visiting the *boucherie, charcuterie, boulangerie, pâtisserie, épicerie, laiterie, fruitier* or *le marchand de vin*. All of them—the butcher, pork butcher, baker, pastry and cake shop, the grocer, dairy and cheese place, fruiterer and the wine merchant— were all within a few minutes' walk. Many of the owners became my friends. What is more, they even liked meeting Australians and other foreigners who were not exactly fluent in French … at least they *said* this about my house guests. The same house guests enjoyed the village atmosphere as much as I did.

Like all apartments in France then, and still in some now, there was a resident concierge. I liked this system. In spite of the fact that they knew practically everything about one (they delivered the mail, took all deliveries, saw who came in with you, saw who left during the middle of the night and so on), they were protection from any unwanted droppers-in. No one could come up to my flat without the concierge telephoning me, saying who it was and did I want to see them? All I had to say was 'Madame Scotter is not here' and the caller would be told no one was in. Remember, there were no mobile tele-phones then, and no one could get in by pressing a buzzer. The concierge ruled the whole block, so it was prudent to have him or her on side. Happily, I managed this.

My Paris job involved quite a bit of travelling—to Italy,

to Switzerland, and to the important textile companies in the north and in the eastern part of France. No hardship to me, as I just adored the European trains, which *always* ran to schedule and provided good meals. I particularly loved my visits to Mulhouse, close to the frontiers of Switzerland and Germany ... partly because, for me, people make places and two of the textile tycoons in that area became good friends (as did their families), but also partly for the beauty of Alsace with its pine-clad Vosges mountains, its quaint old picturesque villages (my favourite being Colmar) and the chance to indulge in what I think even Robert Carrier would describe as some of the great dishes of the world.

Many weekends were spent riding in the forest of Fontainebleau which is only about fifty-five kilometres southwest of Paris. I would drive out there with a beau of mine, Jean Marc Boudoin, who stabled his horses there and we would stay overnight in the forest village of Barbizon. Often, during a winter weekend *in* Paris, I would be watching a rugby match with André Courrèges and his friends from the Racing Club de France (yes, this designer from the Basque country was a highly respected fly-half); and during summer, as I was a member of the Polo de Paris, I'd watch polo at the Bagatelle. Getting to an Anglican church was a bit of a problem, so I would pretend to be a Catholic and pop in to one of theirs, especially if I knew that visiting chums wanted to see the inside of Notre Dame or the Madeleine. While I never understood a word of the services (which in those days were in Latin), I felt perhaps the Almighty would still hear my prayers and not be offended. After all he is God to all, *n'est ce pas?*

Although the Metro was a mere hop, skip and a jump away, and a *stationnement de taxi* (permanent taxi rank) was directly opposite the entrance to number 33, I would often enjoy the thirty minute walk from the avenue de Villiers to the Place de l'Opéra. My office was in the Rue de la Michodière, a tiny street close by the Paris Opera house. I'd lunch each day in one of the many inexpensive excellent bistros nearby— unless entertaining American, French, English or Australian clients of Joseph Bancroft, when we would go to one of the many famous restaurants (as expected!). I should, however, remind you, dear reader, that at the time Paris was not an expensive city, the franc was low and I was being paid in American dollars with a generous expense account.

Inevitably when people know that one has resided in both London and Paris for a few years, they quiz one on the difference between the English and the French. My response has always been to quote the wise words of William Hazlitt, who way back in 1823 said: 'The difference between the vanity of a Frenchman and an Englishman seems to be this: the one thinks everything right is French, the other thinks that everything wrong is not English.'

In 1962 the basics of everyday living changed somewhat when I returned to live in Australia. Instead of a view over rooftops around the Place Malsherbe to Montmartre, my sitting room window framed an extensive view of Sydney's magnificent harbour—right to the famous bridge. My apartment at 39 Wolseley Road, Point Piper, was not within easy walking distance of any shops. The nearest village, if I may describe it as such, was Double Bay, which (luckily) was on my way to and from work. A car was a necessity, and I bought a nifty Austin Mini. For a while I wondered why drivers seemed to slow down when they observed me behind them, until I discovered that the colour and make of my car (robin egg blue) were the same as those used by New South Wales under-cover traffic police.

This Sydney apartment was quite spacious, and an easy and pleasant place in which to give cosy dinners—which I liked to do once a week. I really enjoyed entertaining at home (still do!), as long as I had someone to provide tender-loving housework, which I'm not particularly keen on. As for shopping, this had to be well organised and relied mainly on telephone orders to be picked up from Dean's Delicatessen in Double Bay on my way home. When anyone asked me what I missed from Paris or London, I would say 'some special friends, the odd lover, and the proximity of mundane shops and fresh food markets' (reminding you, dear reader, that I am talking about thirty years ago).

Weekends in Sydney were absolute bliss. For me they needed to be. As already mentioned, my work as editor-in-chief of *Vogue* and *Vogue Living* and director of Condé Nast was exciting and challenging. Although it may sound like one of those 'glamour' jobs, believe me it was jolly hard work, so I appreciated enormously the chance to spend restful weekends sailing on the harbour with friends who owned pretty sleek yachts, conveniently kept at either the Royal Sydney Yacht Squadron at Kirribilli or the Cruising Yacht Club at Rushcutters Bay.

Also appreciated were days spent just lazing and lunching with others around a swimming pool. 'Lazing' is the correct description: I never got wet—I cannot swim.

Routinely each Sunday evening I dined with Frank and Florence Packer in Bellevue Hill. Sometimes the party would include a visiting VIP, other times it was just their family and good friends. I deeply valued my close friendship with Florence in particular. The fact that I had enjoyed a romantic flirtation with her husband well before they were married never worried her. Florence has always been a sophisticated 'continental' woman.

I thoroughly enjoyed living in Point Piper for nearly ten years. And I should point out that this was the second time I had been a settler in Sydney: before going to Paris in 1958 I had had an apartment-cum-office in Potts Point for some years. It was in Wilde Street at the bottom of Macleay Street, on the fringe of the Kings Cross area, which in those days was an intriguingly attractive village—not an iota of sleaze! This was a very happy time, distinguished by my first liaison with an Italian, Ettore Prossimo, who owned the Buona Sera restaurant in Macleay Street. This lasted nearly two years (me—not the restaurant).

Sydney is still one of my favourite cities in the world. However, when I eventually planned to return to live in Australia for good (after the death of my parents), I decided to make Melbourne my home. This decision was *partially* governed by the fact that, while on holiday from the UK in 1979, I had seen an elegantly converted old stable. It was tucked away up a lane in South Yarra and the high cathedral type ceilings made it appear larger than it really was. It had an open plan living/dining/kitchen area, super bathroom–dressing room, a small study, and a mezzanine bedroom ... very much in the style of some apartments I had seen in

Manhattan but with something more: two tiny easy-to-maintain courtyard gardens. I fell in love with the place, bought it and lived there for thirteen years.

But I had other reasons for choosing Melbourne. After living in London and Paris I felt that the lifestyle was going to suit me. I'm not exactly a lazy person but I do like to simplify my life, and for me Melbourne is a *convenient* city. All the things I enjoy seeing and doing—such as the opera, ballet, theatre and art galleries, eating out, shopping, even watching cricket—are conveniently reachable if one resides in an inner suburb. I even find the tram system reliable, and thanks to Victoria's premier, Mr Kennett, there is a quality taxi service in Victoria (I do not own a car). I am not particularly keen on hot humid summers. I do enjoy a changeable climate (even when all four seasons arrive on the same day, which often happens in Melbourne) and the opportunity to wear winter clothes. For some curious reason I feel my winter wardrobe is far more chic than my summer gear. After London and Paris, Melbourne winters seem short and are quite mild. (Which reminds me: when I was living in Europe umpteen Aussie visitors to London would ask 'How can you bear to live in this lousy climate?' My reply: 'I did not come to London for the climate.')

In January 1993 I moved from South Yarra to what I call 'the village' of Albert Park, another suburb of Melbourne. A famous old building that had begun life as a private hotel, and now housed uninteresting offices and two restaurants, was being cleverly converted by Peter de Campo and his brothers to contain a few elegant apartments. Long before completion, amid all the constructional chaos, John

Truscott came with me to endorse my choice of one that I thought had great potential. It had the same spacious open plan feeling of the stable and very high ceilings, and its design and size were perfect for my paintings, my library of books, and all my furniture. No garden—but the bonuses were top security, brighter and lighter rooms with views, a much larger home office-cum-study, plus what is rare these days: a well designed walk-in pantry adjacent to the kitchen area. I find this not only a gem for extra storage of glasses, china and wine but perfect for hiding pre-prepared food such as salad, pudding or cheese platter when giving a dinner party.

Albert Park is unique. I adore the place and hope the village-like atmosphere never changes, nor the friendliness of the people in the shops and amenities. In a way I am reminded of living in Paris, where in each *'quartier'* one can buy *all* everyday needs within a short walking distance. I have accounts with the Villagio Delicatessen and Mandile's Foodtown (both will deliver if I am lazy), also with the Gourmet Bottom of the Harbour fish shop who incidentally (again if I am feeling lazy) provide what must be the best fish and chips in the southern hemisphere. The Fruit Palace next door has top quality fruit and vegetables of almost every kind at quality prices, and people come from afar for their fabulous choice of fresh flowers at amazingly inexpensive prices. Browns nearby has fresh bread twice a day, the local post office has the friendliest efficient staff, and there is a laundry that washes and irons my embroidered white-on-white sheets and pillow cases—and that certainly simplifies my life! So does the fact that at Bis Bas, the hardware shop, you can buy a single nail or screw if that is all you want, and Tony (son of the owners) patiently copes with any idiot like me who cannot even change the batteries in a tiny radio. I would award 10 out of 10 for service and kindness to the Dundas Place newsagent, Travel Avenue, Craven's Pharmacy, Bertie the Bargain Butcher, plus two favourites: The Avenue Bookshop and Links of London (a replica of their Jermyn Street premises in London.) Oh, and this is important for me as I get older: the parish church, St Silas', is also within walking distance, as are the beautiful public gardens of St Vincent's Place. At weekends it is a joy for me to visit the South Melbourne Market a short distance away, collected and brought home again by two dear friends, Jeremy Vincent and Howard Neil.

Reminding me again of the 17th arrondissement in Paris, there is a variety of good eating places close by. Inevitably owners and chefs can change but I fervently hope that Josef and Eileen Fiederling never leave my favourite 'local': their Vista Bar and Bistro in Bridport Street. Other advantages of this village I love are that there is no noisy through-traffic problem, and it is so close to the city and the bay. The Number 1 tram which passes through the city along Swanston Street and St Kilda Road stops within metres of my door or, by walking four minutes, I can catch the light rail Number 96, which goes right up Bourke Street, Melbourne's central shopping mall.

I seem to have elaborated more about living in Melbourne than in London, Paris or Sydney. But this confirms my agreement with E B White: As a settler I am passionate about Albert Park. Mind you, if I were a rich ma'am, I would also be passionate about owning a small hideaway in Paris and another in New York! Wouldn't we all?

No matter what accomplishments you make, somebody helps you.

**Althea Gibson**

# Not the Last Instalment

I have heard it said that an autobiography is rather like an obituary in serial form but with the last instalment missing. I hope no one minds if I end this book by describing my seventy-fifth birthday party—while I am already making plans for celebrating my eightieth! Who knows, the missing instalment might be the start of another book ...

Believe me, I spent a lot of time planning my seventy-fifth birthday party, which was to be a black tie dinner in one of my favourite places, the Peter Rowland Gallery Restaurant at the back of the National Gallery of Victoria. Instead of printed invitations I sent hand written letters which said, 'On Saturday 2 December 1995 I shall be 75 years old ... and I want to celebrate with favourite friends by giving a fun dinner party that evening. You would make me very happy if you would accept this invitation to join me in the Peter Rowland Gallery Restaurant (black tie, 8 for 8.30pm). I have told Peter that my chums are always punctual.'

Most of the energy put into the organisation of the evening came from two *extremely* generous friends, Peter Rowland and Kevin O'Neill. With their staff they took over completely. Peter and I had a meeting early in October at which every detail was discussed, after which, much as I abhor this over-used Australian expression, I have to say that for me this was a case of 'no worries, mate!'

It, too, was a humdinger of a party ... mainly because of the interesting mixture of eighty-three guests, the weather, the scrumptious comfort food and wines, and four very witty speeches. We started with slices of smoked salmon rolled and served with nashi slices, accompanied by a small mixed salad drizzled with lemon and dill vinaigrette. This was served with pita bread baked with parmesan cheese and sesame seeds. For the main course Peter and I had chosen good old bangers and mash (PR's barbecued sausages served with creamy mashed potatoes, pan-fried onions, peas and chutney). For pudding everyone had an individual chocolate brownie cake with the initials 'SS' on it, accompanied by a mixed berry salad and King Island cream. The wines were Katnook sauvignon blanc and Katnook merlot. The Order of the Evening was as follows: Master of *In*formality, Ross Campbell; A Few Remarks, Bails Myer and Leo Schofield; The Proposal (a toast, not marriage), Bill Haffenden.

With my usual Sagittarian luck, Saturday 2 December 1995 was a perfect summer day that produced a warm balmy perfect evening. We all had drinks on the lawn in front of the private entrance to the restaurant until the sun went down, then went in to see (and sit at) all the tables. These were exquisitely decorated by Kevin O'Neill's white gardenias and creamy white rosebuds, bunched into miniature glass fishbowls and surrounded by thick stubby white candles—each wrapped in dark green ivy leaves. My only effort towards the evening was to have planned the seating arrangements. Happily, these seemed successful ... no complaints! Among the guests I was overjoyed to have a member of my family, my cousin Barrie Peters and his wife Ethna, who came down from Sydney. But frankly, that evening, I felt that *all* these adorable friends at the party were my family. Inevitably there were other special friends who were unable to come that night for various reasons. One of the most flattering refusals was read out by Ross Campbell:

Dear Sheila
I'm very sorry to be missing tonight: but while you're at the Arts Centre playing the Grande Dame of Melbourne society, I'm over at the Hyatt attempting to pass myself off as the Lord Bishop of London. [True.] I was therefore unable to take up Douglas Butler's tantalising offer to turn up as one of your husbands. Or possibly both!
In my absence, I'll leave you with this little poem:

In black and white I'll set it down:
You are an ornament to our town.
Sydney has its garish rotters
Melbourne's pride is Sheila Scotter:
A paragon of manners and style
Always going the extra mile
To get things right or help a cause–
The pleasure's ours, the glory yours.
Always in vogue, the height of fashion,
Oozing charm and civic passion;
The rest of the world doesn't know it's alive
'Til it meets our Sheila at seventy-five!
With loving birthday wishes
Campbell McComas

Ross Campbell, as Master of *In*formalities, prefaced his introduction to Bill Haffenden with a reference to my *Bedside Cookbook*, which was published way back in 1979:

[...] now sadly out of print, but in my view still very much in vogue. Chapter 11 is entitled 'No Fear of Growing Old' and Sheila writes: 'Perhaps it's because I live only for the present that I know I shall enjoy my old age. Like the redoubtable Miss Jean Brodie, during each phase of my life, I've always felt in my prime. Now in my middle age [I was fifty-nine] I thank God for good health and pray that He will keep an eye on me.'

Well, He has, and so has Bill Haffenden, Sheila's very special god-son and friend, one of Sydney's brilliant barristers and a man who, while having an eye on Sheila, also has her totally under control ... Ladies and gentlemen, Bill Haffenden.

Stupid me—I had totally forgotten to get anyone to record the witty, serious, flattering, teasing, loving words in the speeches ... a black mark for the committee of one!

It was during Bill's rendering of 'The Proposal' that I learnt of one of the most exciting surprise birthday presents that I have ever received. A great number of my guests had all contributed (anonymously) towards the cost of a luxurious cruise on board the *Silver Cloud*, which I had planned to join in Singapore in late February 1996. I was absolutely overwhelmed. What is more, during the evening my friend Peter Rowland, who was with his wife Susy, came to me and said, 'Sheila, apart from the usual labour and insurance costs, there will be no charge to you for this evening. It is my present to you.' Again I was stunned by this extra generosity. I already knew beforehand that magical Kevin O'Neill had insisted on donating the flowers, and to this day I do not know why I deserved such magnanimity.

I was almost in tears when I went to the microphone to say thank you in words that (from memory) were totally inadequate. I do recall saying that I was the same age as Qantas, the Pope (John Paul II) and Prince Phillip, and probably older than most people in the room. I also reminded my chums that, as a senior citizen, I was born before the pill, frozen foods, pantyhose, dishwashers, tumble dryers, electric blankets, Kleenex, ballpoint pens, and tea bags. Come to think of it, apart from the pill, which at my age is hardly a necessity, I am wondering how I would manage now without some of the aforementioned items which I take for granted. I wish I had thought of telling them that, in my youth, cricketers did not play in coloured pyjamas, smoking was fashionable but grass was for mowing, hardware came from ironmongers and software was not even a word. Perhaps I did ... this was a pretty emotional part of the evening for me and I was terribly nervous. Not for long, happily, as soon people started table swapping, some started dancing and the party was, as the young say, 'swinging'.

I felt loved and blessed to be celebrating this superlative evening with such adorable friends.

P S I have kept the invitation list. It will be jolly useful at the planning conference for (God willing) my eightieth!

# Postscript

I pay special tribute to some gentlemen with whom I have enjoyed breakfast:

    Mr Claude Alcorso
    Mr Geoffrey Batten-Pearce
    Monsieur Jean-Marc Baudoin
    Monsieur Sandy Bertrand
    Captain John Cockburn
    Mr William Cussen
    Mr Desmond Daly
    Mr Bernard Goodman
    Mr John Greer
    Sir Anthony Griffin
    Mr Martin Harding
    The Rt Hon. Harold Holt
    Commander David Kirk
    Mr Alan McIntyre
    Sir Brian Murray
    Sir Frank Packer
    Sir Ian Potter
    Mr Patrick Preston
    Signore Ettore Prossimo
    Mr Derek Roberts
    Monsieur Gilbert Rubod
    Mr Hans Rueb
    Sir Robert Southey
    Mr John Truscott

# Index

Sheila Scotter M.B.E.
At Home

R.S.V.P.

14TH FLOOR
SUPERANNUATION BUILDING
32 ST. GEORGE'S TERRACE,
PERTH
6000
WESTERN AUSTRALIA

Personal from:
HON SIR CHARLES COURT, OBE, MLA

25th February, 1977

Dear Sheila,

As soon as I saw the large bold handwriting I realised it could be
..... Scotter!

... Australia

THE PEOPLE OF DARWIN

AUSTRALIA HOUSE
STRAND
LONDON WC2B

English
National
Opera

Corporate
Membership

English National Opera exists to ...
opera to hundreds of thousands ...
and for many of them a visit to ...
is their first introduction to o...
of performing opera sim...
English helps many new...
many habitual op...
understand...

Although ENO ...
assistance f...
Britain and ...
it needs ...
It is to ...

Corp...

The Lord's Taverners Australia
Patron and Twelfth Man H.R.H. The Duke Of Edinburgh, K.G., K.T.

Victorian Branch
President: Dr. John L.K. Chairman, Queens Hide

EMBASSY
OF THE
UNITED STATES OF AMERICA
Canberra, Australia

December 6, 1967

Premier of New South Wales        30th June, 197...

Dear Sheila,

Thank you for your nice letter of 25th ...
Mollie and I both appreciate your kind thoug...
inviting us to the Bugger Party after the Ope...
It really was a night to remem...

... notes submitted in th...
... given very close con...
... committee which I con...
... Variety...

The
Australian
Ballet

Please keep 2nd December free!

... the kindness and generosity of Mr Willi Merdin o...
... Park Hyatt Hotel, there is to be a very special
... which the entire proceeds will be
... ner from which the enti... overlooks the (fa...
... 2nd December, 1991 to the
... so far

The Silver
Jubilee
Gala

POLO DE PARIS
Mademoiselle Sheila
Scotter
MEMBRE 1969
TENNIS No. 196    P

Gala '78
March 21 1978

Executive Committee
...

Chairman of the Gala Committee
Vice-Chairman: The Lady Lilian Mountbatten Fox

Advertising Sub-Committee
...

... Opera & Sadler ...
Benevolent

Registered Charity ...

from the editor of
VOGUE

CHANEL
BOUTIQUE

WE ANNOUNCE A PRICE REDUCTION
ON SHOES AND SELECTED ACCESSORIES
FOR A LIMITED PERIOD

SUNDAY 2nd ...

THE SIR ROBERT MENZIES ME...
President The Lord Hom...

GALA
'76

English National Opera
at the London Coliseum

CHAMBRE SYNDICALE
DE LA
COUTURE PARISIENNE
...

PRINTEMPS-ETE
1969
RELEASE DATE 1st MARS
N° 8765

BUCKINGHAM PALACE

17th August, 1962.

Dear Miss Scotte...

Commander ...
Holiday and ...

English
National
Opera
Appeals
Committee

The
Australian Ballet
Foundation
Chairman: Trustee: K. F. Cox

THE
DAME JOAN HAMMOND
AWARD

1990 GALA DINNER

2/81